Inspiring Teens Through Social Skills

Providing help and knowledge to be confident in the crowd
and attract true friends

Roundhill Press

© **Copyright 2022 - All rights reserved.**

The content contained within this book may not be reproduced, duplicated or transmitted without direct written permission from the author or the publisher.

Under no circumstances will any blame or legal responsibility be held against the publisher, or author, for any damages, reparation, or monetary loss due to the information contained within this book, either directly or indirectly.

Legal Notice:

This book is copyright protected. It is only for personal use. You cannot amend, distribute, sell, use, quote or paraphrase any part, or the content within this book, without the consent of the author or publisher.

Disclaimer Notice:

Please note the information contained within this document is for educational and entertainment purposes only. All effort has been executed to present accurate, up to date, reliable, complete information. No warranties of any kind are declared or implied. Readers acknowledge that the author is not engaged in the rendering of legal, financial, medical or professional advice. The content within this book has been derived from various sources. Please consult a licensed professional before attempting any techniques outlined in this book.

By reading this document, the reader agrees that under no circumstances is the author responsible for any losses, direct or indirect, that are incurred as a result of the use of the information contained within this document, including, but not limited to, errors, omissions, or inaccuracies.

A little gift to our readers!!!!

50 SELF-ESTEEM BUILDING QUOTES

To get this free gift just go to roundhillpress.com or visit us on Face-Book at Roundhill Press.

Table of Contents

INTRODUCTION 1

CHAPTER 1: UNDERSTANDING WHO WE ARE 5
- The Exclusivity of an Adolescent's Social Life 7
- Teens and Empathy 18
- How Parents Can Help 20
- Personality Types 26
- Myers-Briggs® Personalities 26

CHAPTER 2: MY BODY 41
- What Changes Can I Expect? 41
- Food For Thought 44
- The Hydration Station 47
- Bad Habits 48
- Physical Fitness 50
- Sleep Patterns 51

CHAPTER 3: PREPARING OURSELVES 53
- Tips For Parents 53
- Effective Communication 54
- Prior Planning and Preparation Prevents Poor Performance ... 59
- Organizing Life 61

CHAPTER 4: WHEN WE PRESENT OURSELVES 65
- The Intro 66
- Social Cues 68
- Body Language 72
- Listening Skills 75
- The Art of Conversation 77

CHAPTER 5: THE DO'S AND DON'TS 83
- PROPER ETIQUETTE 83
- BOUNDARIES 84
- EMBARRASSMENT 87
- SELF-CONTROL 90
- SELF-AWARENESS 92

CHAPTER 6: THE OTHERS 97
- WHAT DOES BULLYING MEAN? 98
- THE BULLY CATEGORIES 100
- TACTICS USED TO BULLY 103
- TROLLS 108
- SOCIAL MEDIA 110
- BODY IMAGE 113

CHAPTER 7: RECOGNITION 117
- EMOTIONAL TRIGGERS 117
- ANXIETY 122
- STRESS MANAGEMENT 125
- JUST CHILL 129
- POSITIVE THINKING 133

CONCLUSION 135

REFERENCES 138

Introduction

A typical teen mom's story: "John, what would you like for dinner?"

John: "Whatever…"

Mom: "What does that mean?"

John: "It means whatever! Leave me alone, I'm busy!"

Mom: "Sigh…"

It's true that most teenagers don't listen to adults. While it's purely a part of their developmental stage where they want to exercise their own freedom and independence, some teens start to fail at basic life etiquette or social skills, indicating that they need some assistance. What parents teach their kids during their younger years stays rooted in their minds for the rest of their lives. Some adolescents require that extra push to learn proper social skills and might need some training to feel confident around people, so they don't struggle to find their place in the world.

If you are reading this book, you are either a teen struggling with social skills or a parent of one. If there is anybody that knows how tough it is to understand the communicative nature of adolescents, it is me! I had a difficult time as a teen but managed to grow up into a successful, friendly, upstanding member of society. We can all do it.

As a teenager, you are already confused and uncomfortable with your looks, all the changes to your body, cliques, and peer pressure. So, the last thing you need is to still worry about fitting in among your schoolmates.

Social skills are one of the most crucial skills kids, and adolescents develop because they generally predict how we are going to build deep, meaningful relationships in the future.

When we reach adolescence, we have to deal with rejection, bullies, and conflict. Our fears of complete social isolation can lead to feelings of anger, depression, and anxiety. This may cause us to perform poorly in our academics, and it's very important to address these issues as soon as we notice them.

You need to generate some kind of plan to address and improve any social skill challenges. This will help you to start feeling better about your situation and yourself.

Plus, if we leave any challenges related to social skills and interaction unaddressed, they will persist as we grow up. Eventually, they can become so problematic that they have a major impact on our general day-to-day interactions, our academic performance and ultimately cause more difficulties when we reach adulthood.

Before you curl into a ball, stressing how you are going to fix these issues, let me assure you that I truly believe it is absolutely possible for any teen to learn basic social skills. You just need the right tools for the job!

When learning the essentials of becoming socially skilled, you must try to figure out which skills you are lacking. Remember to aim for desirable behaviors; in other words, focus on behaviors you want to change and get better at instead of beating yourself up over the ones you don't feel good about. For example, it's good to learn the tools to start a conversation instead of running away from someone because you just can't find the right words to say to them. It is also crucial to practice the things you are taught. Social skills are complex, and it will take time to master.

For many teens, that feeling of total disconnection among their peers is just a phase and part of their development. Still, there are some who struggle to build proper communication skills, especially in this day and age where kids are growing up with technical gadgets, learning to communicate through a screen, using shortcuts, and texting to talk to others. This makes face-to-face interaction extremely difficult. We have over adapted to this techno world of ours, and now we need to re-adapt to build healthy relationships again.

The question is, where in the world do we start? How do we connect with others, especially in ways that will benefit our current and future relationships?

We need to break down our walls, uncover our emotional triggers and learn all the necessary skill sets to move us forward in life. We have to become aware of our environment, and we must start to recognize those ever-important social cues we sometimes miss completely. Additionally, we must bulk up our conversational abilities to make us a bit more comfortable being in any type of social setting. Some of us might need advice on how to build our listening skills and read people when we interact with them.

The great news is that if you can identify your issues and practice how to rectify them. This book can be a great tool to guide you in the right direction so you can handle yourself in any social situation with all the necessary advice when things go completely wrong. It will teach you to never beat yourself up or think that you are worth less than anybody else.

This must have read will take you on a journey, giving you the much-needed insight to how your mind works, what physical changes you can expect and getting you ready to participate in any social event. Find all the tools needed to help you with your anxieties, getting rid of bullies, how to handle yourself on social media and much more.

The great news is that you can identify your issues and practice how to rectify them. This book can be a great tool to guide you in the right direction so you can handle yourself in any social situation with all the necessary advice for when things go completely wrong. It will teach you to never beat yourself up or think that you are worth less than anybody else.

In the end, it's all up to you to rectify the problems you are facing because only you know what they are. If you feel your issues could be deep-rooted troubles that this book does not cover, you might need further assistance in dealing with these matters, so we encourage you to talk to one of your parents, a guardian, friend, teacher, or a qualified professional.

Chapter 1

Understanding Who We Are

It was my first day of High School, and we had to introduce ourselves to the rest of our class. My surname started with an A, so I was first up. I thought of something clever to start off with, but as soon as I opened my mouth, I blurted out a few words while staring at the floor. I can't even remember what I said, but I felt so stupid, and any chances of sounding funny or intelligent flew out the window.

I hastily took my seat; my heart felt like it was going to explode. I was utterly embarrassed and super self-conscious about how red my cheeks must have been as I felt like my face was on fire! For weeks I pondered how stupid I must have looked and how dumb I sounded. I must admit, I did cry a bit and lost a good couple of nights' sleep. I would lie awake wondering, how many people noticed? Who would want to be friends with a loser like me? Am I going to walk around being seen as the awkward one for the rest of my high school career?

Even though mumbling and becoming tongue-tied in public can be very embarrassing for people of all ages, events like these where we are judged or evaluated by others on a social platform can be experienced as extremely intense and can haunt us tremendously on an emotional level during our teenage years.

It's an undeniable fact that peer and romantic relationships become one of the most significant features when we hit puberty. They have a newfound motivation to relate socially to others, have a high social ranking, and be part of the "in" crowd.

We become accustomed to processing information related to general social assessments, and they are more emotionally reactive to obvious cues suggested by peers regarding their inclusion or exclusion in certain social circles.

We also become more in tune when it comes to instances of actual or supposed social evaluation where we feel we are being "studied" by the rest of the adolescents in the group.

Some people can be very emotional about what others think of them. This can sometimes lead to overthinking as well as hours of assumptions as to what others' impressions of them could be.

These heightened emotions are known as social sensitivity, and we hope to explore this term to better understand the cerebral and emotive parts that make up the teenage brain.

The Exclusivity of an Adolescent's Social Life

During our teenage years, we begin to strive for our own independence and find where we "fit in" or belong in the world. We become more detached from our parents and more attached to our friends. This is because we are on our way to adulthood and want greater freedom. Suddenly our social lives take center stage, and everything we do, wear, say, or feel revolves around it.

We also begin to become more accustomed to digital communication with a higher frequency of online gaming, exploring the Internet, text messaging, and using social media platforms.

Teens don't just engage more regularly with their peers; the depth of their emotional connections' increases, and they value their newly formed bonds also way more. During childhood, our friends were seen as playmates, but the overall reason for social relationships tends to shift more towards intimate platonic and romantic relations during adolescence.

Social experiences become more constructive, but they also tend to be in a state of constant change as they make close friends quite fast but can drop their bestie just as quickly.

Finding out that we are perceived as low on the social ladder can make us react with great emotional sensitivity, especially if this information is mostly negative and comes from people we deem important.

How Teens are Wired

After facing adverse social feedback, many teens have a major drop in mood and a massive rise in anxiety. Why does their social status mean so much to them? This is because teens' brains differ slightly from children and adults during puberty.

Teenagers tend to use their medial prefrontal cortex more than adults and the "regulatory regions" of the lateral prefrontal cortex less. Their regulatory circuitry goes into overdrive when processing the emotional qualities of social feedback. All teens' brains are wired this way, and that is why they can become moody, depressed, or fall in love so deeply at the drop of a hat.

Imagine how difficult it must be for a young teen to feel as if the entire world is scrutinizing their every move. They are extremely sensitive and what is worse is that they evaluate themselves constantly.

This makes them super self-conscious, and even without feedback from others, their body's stress systems are permanently elevated. The way their brains are wired makes them feel embarrassed even if someone is not looking at them. It's the fact that people might notice them that makes them so sensitive and self-conscious most of the time.

Their social sensitivity is directly linked to their neural circuitry that assigns value to social-affective information. Their newfound need for independence and social acceptance poses a whole set of trials where they have to navigate their world in very challenging ways.

A teen's brain circuitry has a heightened capacity to notice their surroundings and people more effectively. They learn quickly and adapt swiftly to the numerous social challenges they face, enabling more mature social skills.

Social concerns are one of the main causes of anxiety. Being excluded from their social circle can bring about major mood changes and anxiety disorders that could last until adulthood.

When we hit puberty, we are a ball of emotions. We feel misunderstood and alone. It is crucial to realize that this is not only because our brains change. It also has a lot to do with our hormones.

Interestingly our bodies start changing a few years before we hit puberty, and generally, young girls will begin menstruating by the age of 12 or sometimes younger. This is also the time when our bodies start changing. Girls begin growing breasts, our facial features start changing, and pubic hair becomes visible. Our hormonal changes can take up to three years. When we start noticing changes like these, we are now saying goodbye to our childhood years as we enter a new phase called adolescence. Some girls can start showing signs of puberty at age nine, while boys tend to take a bit longer, reaching the beginning of their peak around the age of 10.

It's important to understand that the effects of our hormonal changes and physical development, which includes our brains, generally begin well before we hit our teens. These effects can continue throughout our teenage years and may influence our cognitive behaviors as well as our interactions with others for several years after the initial signs of puberty.

It's imperative for us to recognize the major effects this increase in juvenile hormones has on our neurobehavioral structures as they affect us dramatically. Our hormonal levels go from fairly low to quite high before we turn 14 and are categorized as adolescents.

There are a few reasons why we mention this.

Number One: Puberty is the beginning of the shift from childhood to our teenage years.

Number Two: Biological components like certain hormones can play a major role in the changes of our neural systems during explicit points in our mental development.

Number Three: During puberty, the body has a great increase in testosterone and estradiol.

Number Four: Great shifts in social and affective processes occur during puberty that can play a critical role in predetermining developmental pathways that can have massive long-term effects on a person's health and well-being.

Why should we focus on these social and affective influences of teenage hormones?

All these brain fluctuations and circuitry appear to alert teens to scrutinize their social world. Puberty tends to create a neurobehavioral push toward discovering and absorbing social and affective learning yet also produces some defenselessness towards negative developmental experiences. This can affect teens for many years and can follow them into adulthood.

This might sound extremely scientific, and you are right, so let's simplify things a bit. As kids, our brains grow rapidly, and before we go to primary school, our brains are already 90-95% the size of an adult brain. Although our brains develop fast as children, they still require a lot of transformation before functioning properly and at a mature level.

This intellectual adaptation occurs during adolescence and continues to change until we hit our mid-20s. How fast and how much the brain changes depends on our age, what we experience as well as our hormonal changes during puberty.

Alterations in the Brain

Suddenly our brains form new networks related to the thinking and processing part of the mind. Areas needed during childhood called gray matter are trimmed away, while other connections are reinforced. Our brains are literally changing! The back of the brain gets cropped, so to speak, while the front of the brain, called the prefrontal cortex, gets modified completely. The prefrontal cortex is known as the decision-maker. Its main functions include having the skills to plan and think about the consequences of certain actions. It is also responsible for problem-solving as well as controlling our urges and compulsions. These alterations last until we reach maturity.

Teens are so emotional, impulsive, and intuitive because they depend on their amygdala to make choices and resolve difficulties because their prefrontal cortex is still being altered.

Sometimes we as teens can act quite mature, and then in an instant, we can become childish, and our parents can't understand why we are regressing back to being childish or impulsive. This is because the front part of the brain is still developing. Pathways are not fully created yet, and then our wires become "crossed," so to speak.

Configuring a Healthy Brain

During childhood, the environment we grow up in indirectly influences our way of thinking, how we act, and our feelings. This is vital to a teen's mental and emotional development, so parents are recommended to allow their youngsters to get involved in as many extra-mural activities as possible. If they only sit on the computer playing games for hours, it will have a direct effect on their kids during puberty.

Parents are one of the most crucial elements in a child's environment. How you lead and the example you set have a huge impact on your child and will assist in how their brain develops later on.

So how can you ensure as a parent that your child has all the necessary skills to generate a healthy adult brain?

- Learn behavior strategies for adolescent brain development.
- Endorse proper thinking skills.
- Promote positive behavior.
- Allow for plenty of sleep.

If your child is showing any of the below-mentioned outcomes. Don't fret; it's completely normal during their brain's development.

- Partaking in high-risk activities.

- Expressing amplified reactions.

- Enjoying hazardous behaviors.

- Making thoughtless choices without considering consequences.

What Strategies Can You Use to Inspire Good Behavior and Establish Constructive Brain Networks?

Allow your kid to take healthy risks. Novel, diverse experiences help your child to develop a self-regulating identity while discovering responsible behavior that promotes individuality.

Show your child how new imaginative and communicative outlets for feelings can help you to understand one another. Remember, while the brain is under construction, your child can struggle to express or control their new emotions. Partaking in healthy activities can be a great outlet for teens who are still learning how to control their emotions.

Discuss choices using a step-by-step method. Enquire about the likely courses of action your child can take and explain possible consequences properly. Encourage them to evaluate both the positives and negatives as well as rewards that might originate from their decisions and actions.

Routines allow structure which is crucial for teens. When they know what to expect, they are calmer and more willing to listen.

Offer chances to negotiate when you instill boundaries. While kids need guidance and limits, they also need to know that you trust them enough to make positive choices in life that can lead to independence.

When children show desired behavior, make sure you praise them constantly and provide positive rewards. This helps with strengthened pathways in the brain.

Children learn by watching others. If you portray decent, moral behavior, they will automatically follow in your footsteps.

Establish a tight bond. Your child must have enough faith in you to come to you with any issues or problems they are facing.

Know who your child's best friends are, where they are going and what they are doing.

Your child is just as confused as you are with their new brain developments. Do some research together so you both can understand more about what is happening inside their minds.

Many teens are very passionate about certain activities, especially if it is a social get-together like sports or art classes. Show interest in them and their activities, so they know that you pay attention to their likes, wants, and needs.

Signs of Intellectual Changes in Adolescent Brain Development:

As their brains physically begin to grow and develop, teens will begin to:

- Have rational thought processes.

- Become more knowledgeable and start thinking in abstract ways.

- Understand emotional cues from others.

- Start tackling intricate problems from various angles instead of one-dimensional thinking.

- Having a positive outlook regarding their future.

Showing Support While Your Child's Thought Processes Develop.

Explain how important compassion and empathy are. Have a discussion about how people have different perceptions, and each individual has unique viewpoints.

Make it clear that every action has a reaction. Your teen's mind is still under construction, so they do not understand how their current actions can have future consequences.

It's no use explaining matters with massive scientific words to get your point across. You need to level down to your child's mental understanding. Keep your choice of words simple and easy to understand.

Help your child with the development of their problem-solving skills. Think of a specific action, then try to explore all the problems and outcomes that might result from that explicit act. Continue discussing this problem until you agree on one strategy that can fix things.

The Importance of Sleep During Brain Development.

It's an age-old joke—parents moaning because they can't understand how their teens can sleep for hours on end. The reality is that they need sleep because the body does most of its growth and repair work during this time. Sleeping patterns will change because of hormonal fluctuations as well.

Suggestions to help your teen get ample sleep:

- Create a relaxed, noiseless sleeping area.
- Put away all types of technology at least 30 minutes before going to bed.
- Keep to a schedule. Make sure wake up and lights out are the same time each night.
- Recommended sleeping periods for growing youngsters are eight to ten hours a night.

Beyond Normal Brain Development

Having to face new challenges and major pressures is already stressful for adults. Imagine how difficult it must be for a developing teenage brain. Suddenly they have to evolve from concrete to abstract thinking, and their childhood methods have to make space for a whole new way of thinking.

Every person is unique, and adolescents hit puberty at different ages. The same can be said for their mental development. Each brain grows at its own pace. Some brains have a fully developed amygdala by a certain age, while other teenage brains do not. This creates a discrepancy in brain maturity and can cause adverse adolescent behaviors.

This can affect how some teens control their impulses as well as their moods. It can affect their attention span, and they can have difficulty with self-control and abstract thinking where they fail to understand that their actions now can cause negative consequences for them in the future.

Emotionally stressful situations impact teens way more and can have permanent effects on their mental health as well as the development of neuropsychiatric disorders. Teenage brains are more susceptible to drugs than adults, and they are more likely to get addicted because their brains are still developing.

So, what do parents need to focus on to spot a mismatch in brain and body development?

If your child was never moody and did not display major emotional outbursts, you might immediately think this indicates that something might be wrong. It's vital to remember that our kids' natures are also changing, so there's a fine line between slow maturation and extreme mental issues.

We are talking more along the lines of self-harm, violence towards others, heavy drug or alcohol abuse, and suicidal thoughts or attempts. These types of risky actions and harmful emotions need immediate medical and professional assistance.

If your teen eats regularly, sleeps enough, and has a stable plan for their future with specific steps they are willing and eager to follow to reach this imminent goal, they are on the average brain development spectrum.

If their eating and sleeping patterns are erratic, they self-isolate, have explosive anger outbursts, act out, and lack commitment with zero drive to achieve anything in life, parents may need to seek professional help for them.

Teens and Empathy

As parents, we may sometimes wonder if our teenagers actually have emotions when showing empathy towards others. They might seem "emotionally challenged" and completely self-absorbed, regardless of people being in pain right in front of them! Don't worry. Your child is not going to turn into Hannibal Lector or the Texas chainsaw killer! Remember, your adolescent's brain is still developing, and the area that affects empathy is not fully functional yet.

Adolescents are still struggling with executive functioning skills such as self-regulation, planning ahead, cognitive empathy, sentimentality, and decision-making, so these parts of the brain will take some time before they are fully established.

Teens still need to figure out how to recognize other peoples' points of view instead of their own. They also don't have the ability to identify or respond to others' feelings yet. Solving social problems, managing their own and other people's emotions, and are all skills teens need to learn in their own time.

There are two distinct areas of the brain responsible for emotional and mental empathy, the medial prefrontal cortex and the limbic region. These parts of the brain are responsible for regulating feelings. Mental empathy starts to increase from the ages of 13 in girls, while boys take a bit longer as it only starts rising from the age of 15.

While emotional empathy in girls remains quite high during their adolescent years, it tends to decline in boys because of the surge of testosterone levels in their bodies between the ages of 16 to 18.

Like any other male species on the planet, boys with high levels of testosterone pulsing through their veins have an automatic desire to prove their dominance and exert their power over others. It's easy to see why they would struggle to show compassion and understanding towards anyone else.

Young males are also taught to act tough and fight the need to show any kind of feelings or emotions.

Even if they are beginning to mature and can hypothetically put themselves in somebody else's shoes, they will fear ridicule if they want to act on it, particularly in a group of boys where teasing each other is all part of the game.

We all know that the ones who act super tough and emotionless are actually soft at heart. They want to put up a front for the outside world to protect themselves from being bullied or made fun of.

Eventually, teens get over this phase and will begin to show empathy and compassion. It is crucial that they learn these skills, especially when they have to work in teams when starting their career, as well as understanding others' perspectives when they work in certain areas like HR or assume positions in management.

How Parents Can Help

You can help your teenager to empathize and have a suitable response towards another individual's feelings. It will take a lot of mindfulness and effort to teach your teen what empathy actually is because they still need to develop those areas of the brain until they reach the age of 21.

Don't become discouraged, though. Once your child matures and they do develop decent cognitive and affective empathy, they tend to argue less and have wonderful family relations.

Watching a movie together is a great way to ask your teen how they think the people might be feeling in a sad or heartfelt scene. It might sound too mushy for some, but it's a good method to gauge their level of empathy. You can even ask if there is a specific character that they can relate to.

See if they can associate with people from a different viewpoint! We have already mentioned that kids do what they see, so if you model empathy, sympathy, and true concern for your fellow human being, they will follow in your footsteps.

Helping them problem-solve various situations like being the new kid at their school or being teased will help them understand that their actions can significantly affect others.

Chats and discussions don't always go as you might have planned. You could be bulldozed with answers like "whatever" or "I don't care," but regardless of their response to your questions, know that you planted that tiny seed, and they will think about these things.

Choose your battles wisely and try to have these talks in a safe, neutral setting. Teens can pick up if you have an agenda, and they can shut down quite quickly.

Remember what it was like when you were young. How easy was it for you to show compassion and true understanding towards others? As long as you keep communication open and honest, you will likely win the battle in the end.

Emotional Needs

They throw their hands in the air and roll their eyes. They try and defy every rule and smirk with each suggestion you make. So why would they feel the need to belong? To feel safe and secure? They are now grown up and can fight their own battles after all.

Adolescents might challenge every single word you say or any effort you make to keep them out of harm's way by breaking curfew, hanging with the wrong crowd, or taking ridiculous risks. They even test your boundaries with absolutely everything. But the fact remains that deep down inside, they need you to remain the caring, loving parent who will put their needs above your own and would not think twice to act on their behalf if necessary.

You probably feel confused and wonder how you can find out what they actually need! The best way to keep both parties happy is to communicate effectively so you guys can "meet in the middle" and come to a joint conclusion. Be clear about your fears, anxieties, and worries. Explain your desire to see them succeed in life and what you'd like them to do but be ready and willing to hear their personal point of view too. With proper communication, you will be able to get somewhere with them.

They will never admit this, of course, but what your teen secretly desires is just as much care, attention, and unconditional love as they were given when they were tiny, wide-eyed toddlers.

They want to be noticed, especially on those days when they are irritable, full of mood swings, and hiding away in their bedrooms.

Not noticing their silent cries for attention is one thing, but discounting their feelings because we are irritated by them is something completely different. This can become a hazardous ongoing cycle, where they sulk, we ignore them, so their mood worsens, and we disregard them even further. Eventually, they feel that we don't care enough, which can cause cracks in an already fragile relationship.

Family Time

Teens need time together with their folks and their siblings. They probably would prefer to be chatting away on their phones, playing games, or hanging out with their besties all the time. But they need to understand the real value of "family time." Consider asking them to eat dinner with you, watch a movie of their choice with some popcorn on the couch, or go on an adventurous trip together.

The importance of togetherness has been lost in this day and age, so you have to make it a priority to ensure this bonding time doesn't slip away.

We understand that the pace of life has sped up, everyone has loads of competing demands, and it can be difficult to find the time every single day to bond as a family.

Supper is a wonderful way to gather everybody around one table to talk and connect. Suppose you don't have hours to cook; get the kids involved to cut and peel while you whip up something fast and straightforward. Doing the dishes together can also be one-on one-time where your teen can feel respected and valued, some of their core needs, by the way.

Any human being needs complete relaxation and time out. We are all overstimulated with taking in too much information through our phones, laptops, notebooks, televisions, and other types of technology. We are "wired" 24/7, and many of us never have the time to just switch off and rest.

Our teens get up early to go to school, then rush off to some kind of extracurricular activity, two or even more, while being on their phones in between. They get home, plugin immediately, play online games, spend their lives away on social media, or stare at a TV screen for hours on end.

Our kids also need to keep fit. When we look at some teens, they walk slow, talk slow, and are just slow in general. It can irritate the living hell out of a parent when you are running late for work, and your kid feels the need to dawdle! However, it is vital that they get some sort of exercise even if you have to push them in the right direction. We already suggested one-on-one bonding time during supper, but you can also connect through daily exercise like jogging or cycling together. A hike up a mountain or other types of adrenaline-giving physical activity can actually be great fun for both of you! That is if you can handle these types of nerve-provoking workouts! If you don't think you can rise to the occasion, recommend some club they can join or school sports they find interesting.

Accountability

We all know that adolescence goes hand in hand with conflict when it comes to making choices and taking responsibility. Any teen wants to be wholly independent and believe that they are totally capable of running their own lives. That is until the power goes out or they need more airtime for their phone, of course.

As parents, we want to protect our children even if they are turning into young adults because, in our minds, they will always be your baby. Some parents do everything in their power to control their teenager's life, including their friends, their after-school activities, and staying out with people who they don't know. On the other side of the spectrum, we have parents who don't want any conflict and prefer to let their youngsters do whatever they want.

These are both extremes, and you need to meet your teen in the middle. Give them their independence in certain areas. You can offer more independence when you see that they can stick to your rules. Explain to them that if they can prove that they can be responsible in all aspects of their lives, you will give them more and more freedom because they deserve it. If they do what they need to and you make them feel more liberated, you strike a wonderful balance, and all parties are content.

Acceptance and Respect

Even if you have reached a healthy equilibrium of giving and taking in your household, you might still find some of your teen's choices absurd. They get swamped with all the choices they have to make. Suddenly things go from choosing which spread they want on their school sarmie to what they want to be when they grow up. They have to think about college, what career paths they must take, and some of their decisions might not be what you hoped or planned for them.

Sure, they are inexperienced, and yes, they will probably want to go to the varsity or college where their latest love interest is headed. But regardless of this, you still have to accept and respect their decisions. We are by no means saying that you must leave them to their own devices. You have to guide them and try to steer them in the right direction at all times. But fighting will never fix a situation. Instead, explain your worries, concerns, and recommendations and then listen to their viewpoints. (If they are valid, of course.) Then negotiations can commence, and hopefully, you can reach a compromise. The key to surviving adolescence for both teens and parents is communicating, negotiating, and cooperating. If you can stick to these three components, you will ace this!

Personality Types

According to Susan Storm on phsycologyjunkie.com, there are several Myers-Briggs® personality types.

Every teenager has their own unique, personal struggles, and they all fight these difficulties in their own way. As a parent, you might not understand why your child is taking a certain approach to specific problems you would handle in a totally different way, but it's because of their personality type that they choose that exclusive pathway.

Myers-Briggs® Personalities

We all fall into one of the below-mentioned categories of personality types explained by Meyers Briggs. Once you are more familiar with the various kinds of character traits and how they operate, you might be able to understand your child's personality as well as your own and avoid unnecessary clashes.

ESTJ Teens

An ESTJ (Extraverted, Sensing, Thinking, Judging) adolescent is a real go-getter in life! They love making their own money to prove their independence. They work hard and enjoy the responsibility that comes with true freedom. They are the industrialists and business tycoons. They love being social and enjoy any type of team sports or community-centered activities. They are natural leaders and great life coaches, but when it comes to their own responsibilities, they can become completely overwhelmed with tight deadlines because they say yes to everything and eventually spread themselves too thin. They want to feel secure in their home life, but they also require their own independence. Their "no-frills, no fuss" attitudes can sometimes get them into hot water because they become stubborn and quickly set in their ways. They form their own opinions super-fast, and it could be difficult to get them to see the bigger picture once they have made up their minds.

ESFJ Teens

ESFJs (Extraverted, Sensing, Feeling, Judging) are considerate, reliable, and dedicated. They are permanently involved with school activities and will do almost anything for their mates. They detest disloyalty, betrayal, and bullying. It comes easy to these personality types to cut someone out of their lives if they feel that their values have been violated.

Never try to rush an ESFJ teen. You will just create unnecessary bickering. They do everything at the last minute, which is typical because they want to participate or be involved in absolutely everything in their lives. This can cause them mounds of stress because they are always busy with something or on the run to be somewhere.

Although they have great organizational skills, they struggle with peer pressure and find it impossible to make decisions or to make up their own minds. If you ask them about their dreams or goals in life, they can't answer you because they loathe pressure. They are stubborn and hard-headed and cling to their beliefs without any evidence to the contrary. As parents, it's critical to let them know you love them unconditionally, for who they are and not what everybody else wants them to be. They need to know it's quite fine to be unique and actually admirable to stick to their values.

ENFJ Teens

ENFJs (Extraverted, Intuitive, Feeling, Judging) are usually animated, outgoing, and enthusiastic. They want to help the world with its issues and are quick to mediate when friends differ or fight. They want harmony and unity. They are daydreamers and love adventure.

ENFJs can become overly emotional when it comes to friends and struggle to have their own opinions, preferring to follow their mates' beliefs and values. They can become too attached to friends and might start carrying their baggage for them. On the other hand, if their personal beliefs get violated, they can become tremendously opinionated to protect their views.

Parents of ENFJ teens have to remind them who they are as an individual because they can care so much about others that they lose sight of themselves. Boundaries and self-care are two crucial components the ENFJ needs to focus on. Without proper structures in place, these teens will never learn how to become autonomous.

ENTJ Teens

Our ENTJ (Extroverted Intuitive Thinking Judging) personality types are futurists, very intelligent, and well-liked by their peers. They are self-confident, and their main aim is to become independent as soon as possible. They love a challenge and have fantastic grades as long as their teachers have their respect. They hate the "average" and prefer hanging with people who are a bit strange or "out there." They have their own plan for their lives and will not be swayed to change their minds.

ENTJs are blunt and frank. This can cause ruptures amongst their friends because they have no clue how deep their words cut. They might turn mates into enemies or lose friendships because they are not capable of learning how to be diplomatic or sensitive. ENTJs require freedom and are always out to prove their competence. Many ENTJs are very strong-minded and feel they don't need assistance to achieve success. They are rebellious and struggle with their" one-track" mindedness. They make hasty decisions and can jump to their own conclusions without bearing in mind that there are diverse standpoints.

ENTP Teens

ENTPs (Extraverted, Intuitive, Thinking and Perceiving) would do great in government or politics. They enjoy debating with others and can think on their feet. They always focus on what they can accomplish instead of what they lack in life. Their positive attitudes are addictive, and these adolescents are well-liked among their peers.

They are go-getters, trendsetters, and instigators. They will find the hidden or lost potential in everything. They are world changers, but they need their parents to keep them focused because they have so many ideas and struggle to finish tasks in a timely manner. They are not too perturbed with getting good grades as they honestly look forward to fulfilling their dreams.

They are popular but can find it troublesome to make true friends because they can put people off with their straightforward approach. They will "not soft" soap a situation and like thought-provoking conversations. Teachers and other authority figures usually misjudge them and label them as agitators or ringleaders.

Although ENTPs are full of ideas, they struggle to keep to one project and almost never finish anything. Parents have to push them to first follow through and wrap up one task instead of jumping to the next one, leaving the prior mission halfway done.

ENFP Teens

ENFP (Extraverted, Intuitive, Feeling, Perceiving) teens have a passion for life, love their family and friends, and are absolute visionaries. They have an inquisitive mind and want to be part of every revolution.

They have difficulty sticking to their decisions and struggle to think about where they want to go in life. The burden of making life-changing plans can annoy them because they envision countless alluring possibilities in their lives.

They don't want to be pushed into a corner. ENFPs are very idiosyncratic and want to be the captain of their own ship. Instead of suggestions or recommendations, parents should rather be an ear that listens and a shoulder to cry on.

ENFP teens will place their friends' feelings before their own, and they can become buried in all their peers' problems. They will be wonderful spokespeople and promoters. They believe that there is a solution for every problem in the world. ENFPs require trustworthiness and genuineness, and they love hearing other people's perceptions. Just don't interrupt them or dismiss their views before they have finished their sentence!

ESTP Teens

ESTP (Extraverted, Sensing, Thinking, Perceiving) personality types want to experience life in every aspect. They are thrill-seekers and love adventures. They want to squeeze every drop of pleasure out of every situation and find pleasure in the simple things of life. They are outgoing, fascinating kids with natural charisma, and their friends adore them. They are sports crazy and have a natural talent when it comes to physical activities. ESTPs are generally sociable, easy-going, and crafty individuals.

They are fascinated by physical feats. Their passion pushes them to challenge their bodies, and their favorite pastimes are playing games like football or basketball with their friends. They are not keen to go to school as most classes bore them if no practical element is involved. They are underachievers when it comes to academics but are superstars on the sports field.

They love chasing their own unique interests and are drawn to careers like surgeons because it is a practical job where they can use their hands instead of sitting behind a desk, crunching numbers the whole day. They can make speedy decisions, and although they don't particularly like school, their grades are generally exceptional. ESTPs are not wild or irresponsible, but they do enjoy living their lives in the moment, savoring every quest. They love high speeds and dangerous activities. It is typical of an ESTP to hike across the country or to go explore other countries with only a backpack and a dream. They prefer being their own boss, and many kids become entrepreneurs.

ESFP Teens

The characteristics of an ESFP (Extraverted, Sensing, Feeling, Perceiving) teen include kind-heartedness, being very sociable, and outgoing. They have loads of friends and really care about their loved ones. They worship their high school and will be part of all the activities offered on campus. They will make the most of every occasion and remain eager about life regardless of any setbacks or troubles.

They are unsure of their future goals and can become very stressed if parents ask too many questions about their ideal careers or life plans. They are pretty withdrawn and do not like large crowds. Even though they are generally sociable and know everyone, it doesn't mean that they are everybody's friends.

As mentioned, they want to take part in all the activities but do not enjoy the academic aspects of high school. They prefer working with personalities instead of studying science or biology and will be great doing social work or counseling as they enjoy the psychological side of the world. Their soft hearts can make them susceptible to bullying, and they get hurt quite easily by nasty comments.

They want to be unique and do things their way instead of becoming a carbon copy or the "rest" of the public. They are terrible with finances, and money burns a hole in their wallets. They will spend their cash the minute they get it and struggle with putting some of their earnings away in a savings account.

ISFP Teens

ISFP (Introverted, Sensing, Feeling, Perceiving) personalities are typically caring, sympathetic, and self-regulating. They are your artists, designers, musicians, and sports enthusiasts. They connect with friends and loved ones on an emotional level instead of the corporal world. Many ISFPs become nurses or medical specialists.

They are compassionate, enjoy self-expression, and want their freedom. They can change their minds instantly, and you will never be able to keep track of their racing thoughts.

They are bold and exploratory. They see rules and pre-planning as unnecessary because they enjoy the adventures that are around each corner of their lives. They live in the here and now. Don't expect your ISFP teen to have a step-by-step plan for their future. They prefer to take each day as it comes and will handle difficulties as they arise instead of being prepared beforehand.

They are very ambitious and have strong morals. They value their friendships and are desperate for camaraderie and acceptance by their fellow schoolmates.

They might need additional encouragement from their folks to just "be themselves" and to walk away from destructive relationships. They are not very good with finances and struggle with time management. They enjoy the practical as well as the creative classes in school.

ISTP Teens

ISTP (Introverted, Sensing, Thinking, Perceiving) are hardworking and liberated. They enjoy a diverse range of activities and have no issues getting their hands dirty. They tend to be quiet and prefer to stay in the background instead of center stage. They can sometimes speak before they think, which can get them into trouble, but their comments are generally harmless. They love working with their hands and prefer the freedom of arts and crafts to education and structure. They are not bothered by good grades or happy teachers. They are practical thinkers instead of technical workers. Words and numbers bore them, and they would do well in an occupation where they could live out their imaginations to the fullest.

If you are the type of parent who wants an intellectual child who excels at school, you are going to drive your ISTP teen away. They can make impulsive decisions, and many ISTP children end up experimenting with illegal substances. On the other hand, you do find children who prefer legal thrills like skateboarding and mountain climbing.

INTJ Teens

INTJs (Introverted, Intuitive, Thinking, and Judging) are the "brains" in the class. They are drawn to science and math and excel in almost every subject. They love acquiring knowledge and enjoy anything linked to stimulating their intellectual side. They usually have very good grades if they find their teacher stimulating and interesting, but they won't keep their mouths shut if they do not respect you. This can cause major rifts in their social life because they are seen as nerds. They are practical people and generally don't understand the concept of feelings or emotions. This can make them seem shallow or heartless.

They definitely do not want to be part of any community and will do outrageous things to stand out. They might dress funny or have hectic hairstyles to stand out from the rest of the" sheep herd." Their main aim is to prove that they are unconventional and unique. They will get tattoos, experiment with sex, and use drugs or alcohol. They are incredibly smart but lack the "street cred," so to speak, which makes them targets because they are gullible. They are far beyond their years intellectually but have very little life experience. Some INTJs believe that they are completely capable of living their own life, to their own rules. They are independent from a young age, but it is your responsibility as parents to teach them to respect others and value their opinions. They need to be reminded that they can acquire great knowledge from everyone as there are many diverse personalities out there, and everybody has valuable points.

INFJ Teens

The INFJ (Introverted, Intuitive, Feeling, Judging) teenager is the social butterfly of various personalities. They are very future-oriented and want to find their place in the world from an early age. They are highly creative and passionate about the arts, music, and writing. You get two types of INFJ personalities, those who love company and socializing; and others who prefer their own company.

They do not automatically follow their parents' norms or values and want to make up their own minds. They find it tough to say no to anyone, which can cause major stress for them because they can easily end up with a massive workload. They are also quite impulsive and could be perceived as being irresponsible because they struggle to think long-term.

INFJs love talking philosophy and don't like the shallowness of average teenage ideals, which makes it hard for them to make friends. They so badly want to belong but are never really popular because of their "out there" mindsets. They are extremely emotionally connected to others, which can become exhausting for them, especially when their loved ones are fighting.

They can change their minds as often as you change your socks and might love playing chess one day and want to go kite surfing the next. Parents of an INFJ need to keep in mind that their child is an emotionally impulsive soul and have to continue to redirect their teen back onto the right path every now and then.

INTP Teens

INTP (Introverted, Intuitive, Thinking, Perceiving) teens are known for being quiet, logical, yet independent individuals. They are potential professors and managers. They are extremely intelligent and don't struggle with school tests or projects.

They are not very sociable because they see their peers as one-dimensional and boring. They don't fall for trends and are prone to intimidation and being disliked because they reject the so-called "standard" of normal society. They hide their cleverness and ingenuity from the rest of the world because they feel they are not appreciated.

They are relatively ambitious and determined to spread their wings and fly, becoming fully independent. They will only conform to authority if they respect their views and admire their beliefs. Their high intellect makes it impossible to argue with, but luckily, they tend to loathe fighting.

Although INTPs have superior intellect, they can feel inferior in a crowd. They can become anxious and find making conversation very uncomfortable. They don't like talking about their feelings and can seem emotionally blunt.

Parents of an INTP need to be supportive and challenge their teen's thoughts of subordination.

INFP Teens

INFPs (Introversion, Intuition, Feeling, Perceiving) are the artists, performers, and creatives. They have a wild imagination and try to unearth a sense of purpose in their lives. This can make it hard for them to figure out which career to choose because they want to make a difference in the world.

They have unlimited philosophies and see so many opportunities in their immediate future that they struggle to focus on long-term plans. INFP parents will have to develop imaginative ways to get their teens to find an occupation that combines all their interests. Understanding their myriad of emotions is crucial.

INFP teens struggle the most to leave the nest. Even though they crave independence, they fear losing that bond with their loved ones. They are very private kids, and parents need to encourage them to share their feelings instead of bottling them up. They cannot stand inequality but find it difficult to express their true feelings, which can make them feel depressed and unheard.

ISFJ Teen

The ISFJ (Introverted, Sensing, Feeling, Judging) personality is every parent's dream teen, so to speak. Their homework and chores are always done on time, their homework has been finished way ahead of schedule and they work very carefully with their money. They like smart/casual wear, can be extremely gentle and are very generous when it comes to their friends. They love their community and help wherever they can.

They don't like new challenges and will never take a risk if it's not absolutely necessary. Having said that, they are prone to giving in when it comes to peer pressure because they don't like to "rock the boat." They are people pleasers, which can put them in hazardous situations.

They hate fighting and prefer everyone to be at peace and live in harmony. As they progress in adolescence, they might change into so-called rebels just because they don't want their friends to see them as a softie or a teacher's pet. This is the time when they really need your support and acceptance for who they are deep inside and what they believe.

They can sometimes struggle with concerns about the unfamiliar, which causes great unease in their lives. They want a well-thought-out plan and a clear path to reach their goals, and you must express the fact that you will stand by them 100% of the way.

ISTJ Teens

ISTJ (Introverted, Sensing, Thinking, Judging) teenagers are generally in control and very hands-on characters. They are great money-savers and have no problem studying hard for tests. They prefer a tight bond with one or two close friends instead of hanging with the in-crowd and can be extremely sensitive towards others' emotional struggles. They believe in "saying it as it is" and don't beat around the bush. Their thinking is logical, and they are very responsible. Because of their personality type, they hate thinking outside of the box and prefer sticking to tried and tested formulas. They are risk-takers to some extent but thrive with routine instead of taking chances in unfamiliar terrain. They look for loyalty when it comes to picking friends and consistency in their everyday lives.

Chapter 2

My Body

During puberty, we experience substantial physical changes and loads of growth spurts. As we transition from being a child to becoming a grownup, there are a high number of hormonal fluctuations that occur in our bodies, and we become more aware of our sexuality.

What Changes Can I Expect?

Our sex glands start to release certain chemicals to our ovaries and testes. Girls' and boys' bodies differ, and so do their physical changes. Girls will notice that their breasts are starting to grow, and they can become very sensitive to the touch. Both breasts do not grow at the same rate, so one breast is usually larger than the other.

It's not just boys who experience growth spurts. Girls also go through this. You might notice that your head, your hands, and face suddenly look completely abstract and out of proportion. These physical features tend to change faster than the rest of the body. Your hips will be more prominent. You will notice your underarm and pubic hair starting to grow, and, in the months ahead, that hair will become darker and bushier. Your vulva will enlarge, and you will first notice a transparent discharge on your underwear, which will turn into blood as soon as you get your first period. If your private parts feel uncomfortable, itchy, or sore, you need to tell your parents so they can take you to the doctor. Of course, you are going to be shy. You are just as surprised as the rest of us were when we noticed these physical changes in our bodies, but remember, everyone goes through puberty, and you have to tell your folks if something doesn't feel right down there.

If you are male, you will notice that your exterior genitals, like your scrotum, testicles, and penis, become larger, just like with girls. Your one testicle will be bigger than the other one, so don't stress this is absolutely normal! You are also going to notice that your chest and shoulders will get wider, so your upper torso will look more like an upside-down triangle. Your larynx or Adam's apple is going to be more prominent, and some days you're going to sound like a squeaky wheel that needs oil, but it's all part of growing up and becoming an adult. Of course, your voice will change and get lower, and your pubic hair will start growing and becoming bushier; and darker. Funny enough, teen boys also experience breast enlargement, but it does even out and disappear after a while, so relax. You're not a freak of nature! If you discover that your chest does not reduce, it's time to let mum or dad know so you can go consult a doctor.

As you get older, your beard is going to begin to grow, and you can finally ask your dad to show you how to shave! In the early morning, you are going to experience something called a "morning glory," which is an erection. You can also expect to have wet dreams where you ejaculate because you get aroused while sleeping. Again, there is no need to fear or feel embarrassed. Your body is now producing testosterone, and your testis fills with sperm.

In both sexes, the internal organs grow too. Your bones are going to become sturdier and more solid. Your muscles will increase in size, and sometimes you will feel the aches as they extend, which is known as 'growing pains.' The whole body is changing and improving at different speeds, so don't be surprised if you become a tad awkward, gangly and clumsy. This, too, shall pass.

As if all these changes aren't enough to deal with, you are going to sweat much more, and your face will start secreting oil because you are developing new glands all over. This can lead to body odor, pimples, and acne; we know, two of your worst nightmares! Don't stress, though. Just exercise good hygiene habits and chat to a pharmacist or skin specialist about all the options out there to help with excess oiliness.

Some teens will experience pain in their jaws as their wisdom teeth grow, but we don't all have them. For the rest, you would have lost all your baby teeth which have been replaced with your permanent adult chompers.

Parents,

It is crucial for you to ensure your teenager gets enough healthy food, a good eight hours of sleep, plenty of physical exercise, and lots of love. Remember these physical, mental, and emotional changes will be playing havoc with their feelings and they are going to need all the support they can get.

Food For Thought

While you go through all these major physical changes as a teen, you are going to need added nourishment and sustenance to provide you with the fuel your body requires to grow adequately. You must have heard that age-old joke, where parents moan that their child is eating them out of the house? Well, a big appetite is your body telling you it needs more food, so you eat more.

In your daily diet, you must focus on getting the proper nutrients and vitamins found in healthy foods like fruits, vegetables, protein, dairy, grains, etc., in your daily diet to help your body stay strong. You will become more independent now, so it's important that you make the correct choices regarding food.

Guidelines to Eating Healthy

We know that it sounds boring to eat three meals each day and try sticking to healthy snacking in between, but if you skip meals like breakfast, your body doesn't get the chance to absorb all the required vitamins, nutrients, and supplements it needs to get your metabolism going.

Breakfast is the most significant meal of your entire day. It actually kickstarts your memory and helps you to focus at school. It supplies you with that essential energy source your poor growing body needs to get through a usual teenage day.

Cereals packed with fiber and low in fat are some of the best breakfast ideas. Muesli and yogurt, toast with jam or cheese, and porridge with natural sweeteners like honey or syrup are other power-packed early morning mealtime options to consider.

For snacks, we suggest that you stick to fruits that help cleanse your body and enhance your body's natural defenses.

Dinner time should always include some kind of vegetable or two. Everybody has different tastes, so ask mom or dad to make you veggies you like. To sweeten them, you can add syrup or honey, and if you want to make some vegetables less boring, you can add a little bit of cheese or butter to them.

Eggs, chicken, and meat will help with your protein intake. During adolescence, you need large amounts of protein because it produces red blood cells, which is quite important for girls who have just started getting their periods. Protein helps to keep your iron levels balanced. If they dip too low, you can become anemic, which means your body now has a major iron deficiency, and you can become tired, weak, begin gasping, and experience dizziness.

The natural oils found in fish are vital for your brain to function optimally and promote healthy skin. It's not just carrots that are good for your eyes; fish plays an important role in good, clear eyesight.

We are sure by now you have learned in school that dairy is good for growing bones and teeth, but it also does wonders for your muscles, your heart, and your nerves.

If you are preparing for a big test, you should eat smaller amounts more regularly during the day. It's best to avoid loads of coffee and sugar because you get a "sweet rush" that is immediately followed by hitting a major downer that can make you grumpy or moody. Instead of chips and cookies or chocolate, eat nuts and dried fruits, yogurt, and bananas with a high potassium load.

Another secret for teens with bad skin to know is that chocolate and any oily food types like doughnuts are terrible for acne and pimples because it increases the oil in already greasy skin.

Additional Supplements

We can try to stuff you with as many healthy foods as we want, but there is still no guarantee that you are getting the necessary nutrients to keep growing big and strong. Vitamins and extra supplements are the smartest ways to ensure that you get what your bodies are in dire need of.

A multivitamin is always a good idea. They are crammed with the required amounts and correct dosages a human body needs each day. Magnesium is great for those 'growing pains' we mentioned earlier. B vitamins are a must to boost energy levels and keep you going throughout their day as it's generally a slow-release capsule. Vitamin C is wonderful to keep colds and flu at bay, and a probiotic for good gut health will do wonders as well.

The Hydration Station

Water is the essence of life. No human, animal, bird, bug, or fish can survive without it, and we need adequate amounts of it daily.

Our bodies are made up of water, and we lose large quantities of liquids through urination and sweat. The more active you are, the more you sweat and the more water you need to replenish what you lost. Our minds, muscles, and organs all need water to function accurately. Even if you don't feel thirsty, you still have to drink a few glasses of water each day to remain hydrated.

IF you feel tired, grumpy, or have a headache, it might be your body's way of telling you that it needs water. Camels have humps where they store water, but we don't have an extra supply stashed anywhere. Water is necessary for your brain to function and to help your body flush out built-up toxins. Drinking enough water can also help with physical aches during growth spurts as well as ailments such as heat stroke, so it's recommended that you try and drink more than six glasses of water a day. Milk, juice, cool drinks, and fizzy drinks are not enough to rehydrate your body. Water is also great for acne and pimples. The more water you drink, the clearer your skin can become. It helps with wrinkles, makes your skin smoother, and hydrates your skin.

Small Sips or Downing a Glass

If you have a bottle of water with you during class, you should take a few small sips every now and then just to make sure you constantly hydrate yourself. You can down a bottle of water after intense physical activity. It cleans the system and replaces your lost fluids quickly. In the end, it doesn't matter how you drink it, just do it!

Bad Habits

It is imperative to realize that healthy food equals liveliness. See your body as your 'physical vehicle' and the food you eat as the fuel needed to operate it. You need high amounts of fuel to think properly, move easily, grow correctly, and live life to the fullest. The exact amounts of food, water, and necessary calories needed depend on how old you are, your height, and your activity levels. Our needs will change as we continue to age, and our bodies constantly change during adolescence.

Parents,

We think that today's youths are extremely knowledgeable. They can set up a computer in an instant, recode a program and figure out any type of technological gadget with their eyes closed, but very few are aware of how unhealthy habits can have negative effects on their moods and their emotions. Even though many of them appear to look and act like young capable grown-ups, we forget that their teenage brains are still in their developmental stages.

Bad habits can cause major ructions to teenagers' mental health. Yes, teens' brains are tough, but through the initial formative years, it is vital for kids to develop properly, and some habits can interfere with this process.

Dieting

We all want to look our best, and during puberty, our bodies change so frequently that many teens are not happy with their weight. Some might start to limit their food intake in an attempt to lose that baby fat, but this can be terribly risky.

Many kids try to smoke, take diet pills or develop an eating disorder to lose extra weight, and of course, this will cause havoc with a developing brain. It does not just impact your mental health; it also has a negative effect on your physical health. If you feel overweight, see a professional dietician specializing in this thing to help work out a healthy weight loss plan.

Skipping Meals

Not all teenagers skip meals because they want to lose weight. Some have so many daily activities that their days don't have enough hours to fit three meals in. Some youngsters avoid the lunch hall because of bullying, while others are on meds that suppress their appetites. It is crucial for a growing brain and body to have adequate nutrition every couple of hours and skipping one or two meals a day can cause memory issues, depression, difficulty focusing, and struggles with homework because they can't concentrate.

Junk Food

As our bodies grow during adolescence, some teens have a ferocious appetite, and so many junk food choices at the tip of our fingers can make it very easy for some to become heavily overweight.

The adolescent brain is easily shaped and wired by its environment because of its malleability during the developmental stage. Bad habits like eating too much junk food can become permanent when brain development is complete, and many teens will have issues during their adult years.

Caffeine

Caffeine aggravates feelings of anxiety and can dehydrate the body. One or two cups of coffee a day is fine, but when you guzzle down pots of this stimulant to keep alert and awake to study, you will definitely crash! Coffee plays with your neurotransmitters and can cause mood swings.

Physical Fitness

Recent studies have shown shocking proof regarding fitness among teens these days. According to the Centers for Disease Control and Prevention (CDC), most adolescents aren't getting the correct amount of physical exercise they need. In fact, most teens are less physical than their parents and grandparents. (litlletikes.com. n.d)

They prefer watching television or movies online, playing games, or spending hours on their phones and social media instead of taking part in any kind of outdoor activities.

Physical fitness is so crucial for growing minds and developing bodies. It keeps us fit and helps us to stay healthy and free from illness or diseases. It keeps our organs healthy, strengthens the muscles, and allows our hearts to function effectively.

An active teen will have the right amount of stamina, muscle strength, a healthy mind, and positive self-esteem needed to function at an optimum level in their busy lives.

Of course, not everybody wants to work out in a gym, lift heavy weights, or sweat bucket loads. In fact, we recommend that you go for a nice brisk walk, swim a couple of laps, or go ice-skating. Those guys who enjoy team sports can search for soccer clubs, hockey, or football teams they can join in their area. Horse riding, mountain biking, and trampoline jumping are perfect for young adults who crave more adventurous activities. All you need to do for it to count as 'exercise' is to get your heart rate up, your pulse going faster, and your lungs working a bit harder. A couple of drops of sweat is also not a bad thing!

Sleep Patterns

Sleep deprivation caused by late nights finishing school tasks, doing homework, cramming for exams, or watching YouTube till the birds start singing as the sun begins to rise is the norm for many teenagers these days. The problem is that it can contribute to increased rates of mental health disorders in young adults. Sleep is an emotion regulator, and if you don't get enough of it, you are sure to become crabby and angry at the world for no reason. Some teens also show signs of depression, which affects their whole day.

All these bad habits can affect your immune system your appetite, and harm your health in general. Parents also need to keep an eye on their kids to ensure they live a healthy lifestyle. Don't forget many of them have not been educated around these issues, so it's your duty to correct their negative behaviors.

Try to guide your teen to go to bed at a specific time and wake up simultaneously each day. A nap in the afternoons is also a good idea to charge the body's batteries. Adolescents who are sleep deprived have an increased chance of injuring themselves, having car accidents, and failing their exams because of impairments a lack of sleep can cause. Many young adults are prone to riskier behavior because they struggle to consider certain dangerous situations hazardous. Unwinding before bedtime is vital, so lay down the law by taking cellphones, computers, laptops, and television away an hour before lights out.

Chapter 3

Preparing Ourselves

Having a conversation with friends sounds like a lot of fun, easy to manage, natural and automatic to most. Some teens find it frightening and a total nightmare. In this day and age, most kids are brought up in front of computer screens and cell phones. It's extremely difficult for them to read another individual's body language as well as pick up on another's tone of voice.

Tips For Parents

Parents can help ease their teen's social anxiety caused by a lack of self-esteem by helping them start a conversation, join in a group discussion, or maintain dialog. Entering a group while they are discussing a certain topic can be very intimidating. Help your child to pick up specific social cues like body language, tone of voice, and making eye contact with every person in the crowd.

Starting a conversation can be just as daunting if your teen is super shy and stumbles over their words. A simple 'hello' will usually suffice, but talk your child through the steps to maintain the discussion after the initial how are you. Remind them to give the other party a turn to speak as well as stick to the topic.

Before saying your goodbyes, you need to read the person's body language to see if they are ready to end the conversation. Other skills to focus on include actually listening to the other party. What are they saying? Can they recognize their facial expressions? Are they continuously making eye contact?

It's also crucial to realize that not every discussion has to be a serious debate. When your teen is forming new relationships with potential friends, they can simply stick to small talk and uncomplicated conversations. Topics such as movies, books, music, and leisure activities are great conversation starters and keep things simple.

It will take a lot of practice and tons of different scenarios before your adolescent is ready to tackle the outside world on their own.

Keep them in their comfort zone. Ask your family to join in and start discussions with your youngster to make them more at ease and build their self-confidence.

Effective Communication

Exchanging words is how people communicate with each other. If we can communicate on a more effective level, we will be able to solve any problem, stop and resolve any potential disagreement and understand what both parties are trying to tell one another.

If you suddenly find your mind going blank and your body frozen with fear while trying to have a conversation with someone, there are six crucial questions you can fall back on to refocus.

What

Think of the message you would like to convey to your friend, teacher, or anybody else. Babbling and spewing a couple of words to try and string a sentence together is not the best way to communicate. Rehearse your side of the conversation by asking these four questions to yourself in your mind.

- What do I want to say?
- What is my message about?
- What do I want the other party to take away from my discussion?
- What should my conclusion be?

Why

If we are unsure about the reason for our conversation, we might say something we didn't intend to. This can make our message sound wrong, and the recipient might not be able to understand the context of the discussion. Make sure that you know your message's purpose and if you are talking to the correct person. A few questions to keep in mind:

- Why do I want to say something now?
- Why do I want to talk to this particular person?
- Why is my personal opinion important?

When

The right time, place, state of mind, and mood are so important when you want to communicate something important to someone else. They might be busy with an important deadline, worried about some personal issue, or just woke up on the wrong side of the bed this morning. Reading social cues and picking up on body language will help you to find the perfect time to approach the person. Make sure they are calm and have enough time to talk to you before you just jump in with your speech! You want to make sure that they aren't going to cut you off mid-sentence, so plan your approach meticulously. Three questions to consider are:

- When is the best time to start this conversation?
- When should I approach this person?
- When should action be taken?

Where

Not everything has to be done face to face. Sometimes a message via your phone or an e-mail can do the job just as well as in person. We are focusing on social events, so it might be a good idea to invite the person to a nice, calm place with a relaxing environment. It makes things harder if you are trying to talk about something serious while there are ten kids running around, screaming, or the telephone ringing non-stop! Sometimes it's better to wait for the right moment and place before you start your conversation. It is also recommended that you have some type of backup at hand if the other party wants some additional information or facts. Another friend who can fill in the blanks for you or extra resources to get your point across can be very useful! Before picking the right spot, inviting another person, or sourcing additional info for your cause, here are four questions to keep in mind.

- Where are my sources for my information coming from?

- Where would the ideal meeting place be to have this conversation?

- Where will I feel the most comfortable?

- Where can I get additional information to back my opinion?

Who

If you target the wrong audience, you are not going to get satisfactory results regardless of how amazing your speech is. If they are not interested in the topic, do not share the same beliefs, or have the same morals as you do, the chances are that your plan is going to backfire! See if there are any alternative ways to get your point across that can pique your audience's interest. Don't forget there is more than one way to "skin a cat!"

- Who are the people I want to target?
- Who is going to be affected by my information?
- Who is in charge of this conversation?

How

Finally, you need to figure out HOW you are going to implement your plan to get the person you are targeting to listen to you.

Your message needs to be clear, to the point, and effective. Maybe practice your speech a few times just to get the hang of it before approaching anybody.

We have five questions below that you can answer to make double sure you know what you are going to say!

- How am I going to get my point across?
- How will my conversation affect both parties?
- How can I convince the second party of my opinion?
- How can I communicate more effectively?
- How do my words impact others?

If you have an answer for everything, you can rest assured that these six Qs will help you communicate in a more impactful manner, sending out an effective and meaningful message without stumbling over your words, anybody losing their cool, or boring your target audience to death.

Go on, give it a try!

Prior Planning and Preparation Prevents Poor Performance

The P rule focuses on getting yourself ready before any social occasion or ahead of a stressful situation you know you are going to face. If you prepare properly and to the best of your ability, it makes a huge difference to your overall performance.

Any advancement or progress in life needs adequate planning before you can move on to 'action mode'. Time management is very important, so plan ahead before you just decide to jump in at the deep end of a situation. Write out a schedule the day before you begin your endeavor. As soon as you have written down everything you have to do, it actually clears your mind and relaxes you. This increases your productivity and helps you to think more clearly. Remember, we are not talking about the exact steps you need to take to fulfill your task. We are just working out a plan on paper to make sure that we do not leave any critical details out.

Planning something correctly intensifies your efficiency because you know what is expected from you. By setting and reaching your goals, you increase your self-esteem and enhance your sense of personal power.

Another tip to increase your productivity is to begin your day early but well-rested. The more time you take to ponder your situation, plan your route of action and organize your day, the better your chances are for success. If you are planning to start your day early, you need the necessary hours of sleep to feel energized and ready to tackle any situation. So make sure you catch those ZZZs.

A few moments of silent reflection before you begin your task will ensure calmer, more creative, and clear-headed thoughts.

Focus on your work when your body is the most productive and your mind is more alert. Remember, without a proper plan; you will undoubtedly experience unexpected problems. As soon as you have a plan of action, you can move on to the next phase, which is organization.

There is another set of rules you can interlink with the previous suggestions. Focus on the speed at which you communicate, and don't try to rush things. Monotony is a dead giveaway that you have practiced your words too many times, and the listener will know that there is zero feeling attached to your pitch, conversation, or introduction. If you raise your voice a bit, you will sound excited and will make your listener feel more enthusiastic over the conversation you are about to have. A lower pitch will let the listener know that you are talking about a serious subject. Speak with clarity and make sure that you pronounce your words properly. Finally, try to pause in-between sentences so the listener has time to grasp and take in exactly what you just said. We know that all these tiny rules and regulations are probably scaring you to death, but they are mere suggestions. Once you have them under your belt, your conversations will flow, and they will come naturally to you.

Organizing Life

Now that you are in high school, 'hitting the books' is far more hectic than writing one or two sentences about your dog or a simple math sum. Your homework has increased by a ton, and you need to keep track of all your tasks, tests, projects, as well as the other 110 things you need to remember!

The best and only way to do this is by organizing everything. You might feel overwhelmed and anxious over your workload, but with the proper strategies, you will soon realize that everything has its place, and there is a place for everything! You don't want your mom or dad on your back because you seem disorganized, either. So, this is your chance to show them just how prepared you are for life, independence, and responsibility!

Get a Daily Planner

Your day goes so much smoother if you can break it up into segments. A daily or weekly planner ensures that you write anything important down first. As soon as you have a clear picture of what needs to be done, you can start organizing your day. If you feel that a paperback is too boring or you might lose it, save everything on your online calendar! An electronic agenda also has the pros of scheduling reminders and setting alarms for deadlines, so you really have no excuse to miss anything.

Have Family Meetings

Another good idea is to get your folks onboard by setting schedule checks in advance. Let them have a look at your planner so they can also keep track of your activities. This shows even more self-efficiency, and they will be so surprised to find out how 'on the ball' you are! Have a family meeting where you guys can sit down and discuss everybody's expectations. They might want a certain set of grades on your report card, and you might need a few extra dollars for your empty piggy bank. Come to an agreement and make sure you keep to your end of the bargain so that they can keep to theirs.

Clean Out Your School Bag

We all know how heavy our bags can become over a week at school. We keep on stuffing it full of notes, lunches, extra clothes, homework, books, folders, pens, etc. It is necessary to clean that mess and clear out anything that is not needed anymore! Make it a point to check each pocket as well as all those hidden compartments so you can get rid of all the excess chaos and only keep the absolute necessities.

Create a Workspace

Find a spot in your room or in the family office that you can make your own. This will be your workspace. Make sure the desk is neat and tidy, with enough natural light as well as a comfortable chair to sit on. Pack all your essential homework aids nicely in a drawer or a plastic container so it's easy and quickly accessible. Things like sticky notes, extra pens, paper, various folders in different colors, labels, glue, pencils, and whatever else you feel you might need should be packed into your storage container. A great tip is to use a different colored file or folder for your various subjects to know which colors you need to grab when you are packing your school bag.

When you are organized, you immediately feel more relaxed and ready for your day, no matter what curveballs life throws at you! You will quickly realize how much extra time you have now that you don't have to turn your entire room upside down looking for that pesky pencil case. By not leaving everything till the last minute, you might have some free time to spend with your friends, because you don't have to spend your weekends trying to catch up on a whole week's work either! The best thing about being organized is going to sleep with a clear conscience, knowing that you are fully prepared for the next morning. No more lying awake, rolling around, and stressing about tomorrow because you know 'you've got this!'

Chapter 4

When We Present Ourselves

It's time to explore and refine our overall awareness. Recognize social cues, listen with an empathetic ear, and overall improve on reading people better during our interactions with them.

We still want you to stay true to yourself, so please no fake personality changes, masks, or playing pretend. This chapter is not about fitting in; it's about feeling comfortable in a crowd while being 100% authentic!

Fear not if you feel the sweat dripping from your forehead while you have no clue what to do with your hands when you need to present yourself to new people. We have a step-by-step solution to fix your awkwardness.

There are loads of teens out there who prefer to be a wallflower at a party or social event. Honestly, though, who wants to hide in a dark little corner while the rest of the kids are having an absolute blast? We promise that being shy is no terminal illness, so you won't die from embarrassment. Even though there are numerous reasons why you might feel edgy and uncomfortable in a new crowd, it's actually not the end of the world if you are not as smooth as your friend next to you.

The Intro

When introducing yourself, it's best to start with something easy and simple to remember, so why not just tell them your name? We all have one, and most likely, they are going to respond by telling you theirs. If you feel up to it, but it's definitely not necessary.

Set a Challenge

On the next social occasion, you are invited to compete with a pal to meet two new people at the event before the party is over. It's no use challenging yourself because nobody can hold you accountable. It might feel dumb the first few times you try it, but after a few practice rounds, you will be surprised how easy it is to introduce yourself and ask someone new their name.

Break the Ice

Not everyone has the gift of the 'gab,' and we realize that some people are generally awkward, so the best way to continue with a conversation after initial introductions is to ask a question. If you listen attentively, you are going to pick up several clues about what the person would like to talk about next. In most situations, their expectations are that you will continue with a specific topic by asking a question.

The trick is to get the other party to give you an answer, so guess what? They are actually doing most of the talking! Keep things simple, though, don't ask difficult questions, never talk about politics, and please don't ask them about the weather conditions.

Try a topic like their favorite type of music, songs, and bands, something related to sports, or even the food and drink in their hands. Anything goes, as long as it gets the second party to continue chatting. Another tip to remember is to have a few aces up your sleeve when answering questions. If you ask a question, the person you are talking to is most likely going to inquire about your passions as well, so practice a couple of answers regarding your own likes and dislikes.

Use Comedy

If you feel up to it, you can start the conversation with a funny statement, quote, or fact. Find something amusing and entertaining and memorize it. The next time you are standing alone at the drinks table and someone approaches, go in for the kill! Just try not to forget the punchline!

A quick reminder for you: most kids are just as petrified as you are! They will probably be relieved that someone else is starting the conversation and have been waiting half the night to get someone's attention. They are going to appreciate the fact that you decided to take the risk to chat with them, so take on the challenge and meet two new friends today.

Social Cues

When you chat with someone, both of you use social cues. You might not realize that you are automatically sending out signals with your facial expressions, physical distance, and tone of voice. Picking up on these cues is an unbelievably helpful skill when you're trying to 'read' a person. It can also be a pain in the butt if these skills don't come naturally.

We are going to explore a few obvious signs to look out for that can help you figure out what the person actually means without them using words.

Time to Wrap Things Up

Nobody likes someone who carries on with a conversation even though you have mentioned multiple times that you are in a hurry or late for an appointment. Realizing when you should end the conversation can be complicated. Some people might think that you want to get rid of them if you end your discussion too quickly, while others can get irritated with your infinite blabbing.

So how do you spot the right time to say goodbye? Many people will become fidgety, others might look around them, and some might just come out and say they have to go. Keep an eye out for any uncomfortable silences or awkward pauses too. This is usually an indication that they have run out of things to say.

Staying Alert

Our own nervousness can often make us think that other people might find us boring or dull. Check out their facial expressions. If they are smiling, laughing, and making eye contact constantly, the chances are that they do find you entertaining. Their whole body will be facing you, and their tone of voice will be filled with excitement. They will answer your questions and ask their own to keep the conversation going. If you are struggling to figure out what they are thinking, keep in mind that people who ask questions but don't really listen to your answers are just being polite, and you should cut your conversation short.

Switching Topics

If someone is giving you short answers and trying to change the subject the whole time, it does not mean that they aren't interested in you as a person. It might just mean that they really want to talk about something else. If they end their sentence with a new question, don't jump back to the previous theme; continue with the new suggested proposal.

Swapping

Teens might struggle to include themselves in a conversation, especially if they just entered the room. Allow them to join the discussion by asking them what they think. It is generally noticeable when someone is dying to say something. Their mouth is slightly open, and they will take a deep breath just after you have finished your sentence.

No Means No

Most people find it difficult to say no to someone. Instead, they will make excuses for why they can't stay and say something along the lines of "I'm going to have to take a rain check on that cup of coffee." Many of them won't even use the N-word because they fear rejection from your side. Stay polite and tell them that you can't wait to catch up another time. This will give them comfort that you are not angry or frustrated with them.

The Joke's on You

When you know someone well, it is fine to play around and make jokes with them. Trying to do this to someone you're not familiar with can lead to them misunderstanding you completely! Most of us usually give a sideways glance, a raised eyebrow, or a grin when we are being playful or light-hearted. Some people use humor to put others down, pretending that their nasty remark was meant as a joke. Ignore those childish fools and walk away; this is where your body language can show them that you think they are a jerk!

Notice Annoyance

When a person is irritated or frustrated, they will usually keep their sentences short and to the point, without asking a question to continue the conversation. Look out for sighs and eye rolls. These are clear signals that they don't want to talk right now.

Wanted or Unwelcome

The reason why we are discussing social cues is for you to learn when to continue with your conversation or when to say your goodbyes and move on. There is nothing more frustrating than a person carrying on about something while you have said and done everything in your power to let them know you are "A" not interested and "B" couldn't give a damn.

People who are exhibiting positive social cues have an inviting, comfortable, and friendly attitude. Negative social cues include an antagonistic tone of voice, minimal eye contact, and signs of physical irritation.

Sometimes people are just preoccupied or stressed out about personal issues. It's not always the case that if someone is not interested in talking to you, they don't like you. Before you run away and hide under your bed because you feel like a one-eyed monster who is too scary to be seen in public, find out if their negative social cues are specifically directed at you or if it's a general message. If their behavior is similar while talking to others, chances are that their cues are a general statement, and they might just have a headache or a very bad day.

Rehearse and Prepare

Unfortunately, we are not born with social skills or superpowers. They are life lessons that need to be learned. Check out how people around you behave and see if you can pick up on the gestures they are performing.

It might sound corny but ask one of your family members to help you out. Stick them for a milkshake at your local mall and play the "he said, she said" game. Pick a table and watch them for a few minutes. Try guessing what they are talking about and sum up their facial expressions, hand gestures, and overall temperament. Focus on their eye contact and if they are chatting with a smile or a frown. Tense facial expressions are a dead giveaway that they are not very happy.

My Cues

Observing and understanding other people's social cues is one thing, but what about your own? Now that you have read this small, short cheat sheet of cues, you know what to look out for. So, use these signals during your own conversations too. Make sure that you keep eye contact at all times. Don't have a serious facial frown if you are not angry and try to smile every now and then! A proper conversation is all about give and take. Remember, you will get back what you put out, so keep it friendly and funny if you want playful, informal chatter with your buddies.

Nobody's Perfect

Becoming a social cues master is impossible. Yes, you might be able to notice some signals, but trying to scrutinize every single signal and analyzing each physical movement or facial expression will exhaust you! Don't be too hard on yourself if you miss something. You are a teenager who wants to understand the people around you, not an investigator who has to solve a kidnapping.

Body Language

A person's body language can reveal what they are thinking. The words coming out of their mouths are not necessarily their true intentions, but by spotting certain gestures, you can 'blow their cover,' so to speak.

It's All in the Eyes

Eye contact is the number one giveaway when it comes to sussing out someone's body language. If they can't look you in the eye, they are probably lying, bored or disinterested, especially if they look down at their feet. People who are anxious or uncomfortable also avoid eye contact, so check out the rest of their movements before making a final call. The number of times a person blinks is another clue. An increase in blinking could mean they are being deceitful, and if they are touching their face or looking to the right or left, they are definitely not being honest.

Facial Expressions

A person laughing means they find you funny or are happy and excited to see you. A fake smile can be spotted from a mile away, and you can be sure that the person is not being sincere. Half a smile can indicate sarcasm or doubt. A quick smirk that lasts less than a second typically suggests that the person is hiding something. Tightened lips are usually a sign of annoyance, while a relaxed mouth shows a comfortable, optimistic temperament. Someone covering their mouth when speaking might be a sign of dishonesty.

Head Movements

You can learn a lot from head movements. Someone who nods their head while you are speaking is not just agreeing with you; they are showing interest in what you are saying. A person who nods too often and who looks like a 'headbanger at a metal concert' has lost interest in your conversation and stopped listening a while ago! A head tilted to the side could indicate interest, while tilting the head backward can show distrust and ambiguity. You will notice that the 'bigwigs' or very important people usually have the entire crowd facing them, while the less significant people like the coffee boy or girl don't even get a second glance.

Hand Gestures

Hands on the head or in pockets suggest that the person is nervous or deceitful. Someone supporting their head with their hand on a table shows interest, while holding the head in both hands can mean boredom or sadness. People will hold something in their hands if they want to create some kind of imaginary wall between themselves and the other person.

Arms

Crossed arms have a double meaning. It can be an indication of apprehension, vulnerability, or closed-mindedness, while crossed arms accompanied by a genuine smile and a comfortable posture indicate a confident, relaxed attitude.

The Feet

You are probably completely flabbergasted over the fact that we are mentioning 'footwork!' Generally, a person is so caught up with trying to put up a mask that they completely forget about the lower part of their body. A very interesting tidbit is the fact that people will naturally point their feet in the direction they would like to go. If their feet are pointing in your direction, it means that they hold you in high regard. If they are pointing their feet towards another party while talking to you, they most likely want to rather be chatting to that person.

Proximity

The closer you are to someone, the more relaxed you feel around them. We tend to keep our distance if we are unsure, uneasy, or distrustful. Keep in mind that some people just don't like anybody standing near them, especially if they have anxiety issues, so it's not always an accurate indication.

Mirror, Mirror

The 'mirror effect' involves someone copying another person's body language and behavior. If you think your friend is mirroring you, do something obvious like picking up your drink or placing your arm on the table. If they make the same gesture within ten seconds, they are definitely imitating you. Don't stress, though. This doesn't mean that they are some psycho who wants to get rid of you because they plan to take over your life! They are actually trying to establish rapport which means that they admire you or they would like a close emotional connection.

Listening Skills

Interaction between two or more people includes two integral components, expressing yourself and listening to others. Most of us are great at talking, but we suck when it comes to the listening part. Hearing what someone else says and listening to them are two totally different things.

Why Is Listening Important, You Ask?

- It helps to understand a person's emotions
- It makes others feel valued
- You absorb the information that has been disclosed
- It builds trust
- It helps to connect people and strengthens the emotional bond between them

How to Become an Active Listener

Active listening is yet another skill we need to be taught. It takes effort and a lot of practice. You need to be focused, concentrate on what is being said, and you cannot have any distractions around you.

If you listen closely to someone, you must engage with them by speaking to them occasionally. After they have finished their final sentence, try to summarize what you think they said.

Struggling to Hear

We sometimes have too many things going on in our own heads, and that's why we struggle to listen properly. We might be distracted because we are completely wrapped up in our own problems. We might have opposite beliefs or views or have already formed opinions about something without hearing their entire reply.

Why Bother?

Many fights occur in a relationship because someone didn't listen properly. People can avoid most misunderstandings if the person just heard what was said instead of making their own assumptions. These small arguments are generally not a massive issue, but they aggravate people if you still don't get what they say after they just poured their hearts out.

A person who feels heard will trust you way more because they know that you truly care and are interested in what they have to say. They will open up more and start communicating on a deeper level. As soon as you hear what is being said, you immediately understand that person's perspective, which is crucial to evoke empathy. Active listening improves relationships. It doesn't matter if it's a friendship, romantic, family, or even business. Any relationship is built on trust, and active listening builds that trust.

The Art of Conversation

So, you have practiced your introduction, you have a great opening line, and you are ready for action! You scan the scene for a potential target and find the perfect potential 'new mate.' Your conversation starts off well, and you are just about to pat yourself on the back for effort when you suddenly hit a long pause in the discussion.

You immediately start to panic. What now? Calm down! It's common for conversations with new people to hit an obstacle. Remember, you don't know each other yet, so it's going to take some effort from your side to 'hook this fish.'

You have thrown in your rod, and they took the bait. All you need to do now is reel the sucker in!

Pick Certain Topics Beforehand

You have a lot of potential conversation starters already; you just don't know it! Think of all your hobbies, movies you enjoy, activities you like to take part in your future plans after school, career options, etc. Make yourself a tiny list that you can keep close and read through it before you approach your next social experiment.

Stay Open

Open-ended questions will make sure that the other person must end the silence with an answer. These are questions that need more from the person than a simple 'yes' or 'no.' Be sure to ask them something along the lines of "What do you think of so and so?" Instead of asking, "Do you like so and so?"

Whatever Comes Up

Sometimes you just get stuck and have no witty comment, funny comeback, or interesting question to ask! Well, then you say whatever comes up first in your head! This is called 'blurting,' and it might sound silly, but it actually works! You may even find that you managed to start a whole new conversation!

Leave That Pause

Things were going great, and then suddenly, you looked at each other, and neither said a word. Time is dragging by, and seconds feel like hours! Don't feel obliged to say something if you don't have anything to say. Allow the response to restart the conversation with a new topic even if it feels like agonizing torture. Hang in there and let the silence just be. In the end, the other person will end the awkwardness.

Hooray! You made it! You had your first social interaction, and all your practice, hard work, and extra 'cheats' worked. Now, the only issue you have is to wrap up this conversation in a manner that doesn't make the other party feel unwanted. Any chat can go south if it carries on for too long.

Get Going

Remember we already chatted about body language, and you can use this to your advantage. If you are sitting down, you can stand up and say something like, "It was great to see you again, but I have to go." An honest end to a conversation without any extra frills, bells, or whistles will leave your conversation partner at ease, and they definitely won't take your exit personally.

Steer the Conversation Towards the Other Party

If you do not have the opportunity to make a quick exit, you could always give the other party the option to vamoose! For example, if you are at a party, you can say something like, "Wow, I remember that you love this song! Your feet must be itching to get on that dance floor! I wish I could join you, but I have to freshen up." If they catch the hint, they will probably reply, "yes, let me go show those people one or two of my dance moves!"

The Hand Over

Chatting in a group allows you to hand your partner over to someone else by introducing them and mentioning something they both enjoy or like. This gives them an immediate topic to discuss, and you can be on your merry way without any guilt!

The 360

Ending the conversation with whatever you first discussed is also a good 'close.' You can mention something like, "I can't believe we both came to get the exact same video game!" "I'll be sure to let you know what my high score is.". This specifies that the chat has come to an end and gives you the chance to tie up any loose ends before you say your final goodbyes.

Back To the Future

As mentioned above, you can end a conversation with the initial topic you began with, and before parting ways, you can schedule another chat in the future. For example, you already mentioned that you are going to let them know what your high score is, so now you can end off by inviting them to your place for a proper battle. If you don't want to go that far, you can simply ask them for their number or Email address and mention that you will give them a shout sometime.

Stay Friendly

Even if the person nearly bored you to death, irritated you so much that you almost drew blood by clenching your fist too tight, or gave you lockjaw because you kept on having to bite your tongue. It is just manners to end the discussion with a kind word or a compliment. Say thank you for their great advice or mention that you enjoyed hearing about their latest trip. The point is to leave the second party with a positive impression of you. Who knows, maybe not now, but you just might need their help in the future. So don't burn any bridges if it's not absolutely necessary!

For Pete's sake, don't think that socializing is so difficult that you rather want to stay a recluse at home forever! It's actually supposed to be fun, so remember that part. See each person that you meet as another opportunity to hone your skills, but don't feel like a total loser if everything didn't go according to your well-thought-out master plan.

With sufficient knowledge and practice, you will soon be confident enough to have a chat without even stressing about social cues, body language, facial expressions, voice tones, etc.! Expect every interaction to be unique. We are not all carbon copies, nor are we sheep that follow the herd. You must remain flexible and adaptable to each interaction in every social setting.

It's all about dressing up, showing up, and doing your best. The rest will fall into place.

Chapter 5

The Do's and Don'ts

We all have been brought up with regular household guidelines. Saying please and thank you. Eating with our mouths closed and never put our elbows on the dinner table.

Proper Etiquette

There are a few other important tips to remember when you are in a social setup.

Introductions

You might know your buddy as "Bones," but surely you don't expect your mom or dad to call them that. The rule of thumb when it comes to introducing somebody is to speak to the person you have the most respect for first. In this case, you'll introduce your friend to your parents by saying: "Mom, Dad, this is Edgar, my high school friend. We have math class together."

Eye Contact

Don't you just hate it when you are trying to speak to someone, and they are busy on their phone? Well, you are not alone. Eye contact is extremely important when you are socializing. Don't stare the person down; you are not partaking in a cowboy shootout, and you definitely do not want the other party to think that you are some creep. A good tip is to copy the person you are chatting to. If they make eye contact, follow their lead, and glance to the side, do the same. Just make sure that you are not too obvious. They mustn't realize that you are imitating their actions.

Bad Language

Many teens swear. This is a huge "no, no" in public! Dropping the F-bomb around kids or adults shows utter disrespect, so say things as they are, but don't sour a conversation by using vulgar language. It's inappropriate, uncalled for, and gives you a bad rap.

Boredom

Okay, so you are bored, and you can think of 100 other things you would rather be doing, but yawning out loud is truly just terrible manners. There is really no excuse, so just don't do it!

Boundaries

Think of a boundary as a stop sign at the end of your street, a wall between you and your neighbor's yard, or a moat around a castle to protect the royal family. A boundary is a border or an invisible fence that a person sets up that people are not allowed to cross. Setting personal boundaries is a necessity, especially during adolescence. You want real friends who are willing to look after your emotional needs. You definitely don't need some leech who never takes "no" for an answer or wants to surpass your personal morals and beliefs.

Emotional Boundaries

An emotional boundary is put in place to protect you from manipulation or mental harm. People out there love to use others, and an emotional boundary ensures that people understand who you are, what you believe in, and how you feel. See it as a safe space between you and the rest of the world.

Any kind of relationship needs emotional boundaries. It shows that you know one another's limits and that you respect them. Telling someone that they are crossing your boundaries doesn't make them bad people. It just reinforces the trust you put in each other, and if they really are your friends, they will respect you for speaking up.

Healthy Boundaries ensure that you trust, respect, connect and appreciate each other. Teens who struggle with boundaries will allow their friends to direct their lives. They will fall victim to people planning to use them and fall apart if a friend disagrees with their views. They will do anything to please everybody, even if it's against their beliefs and morals.

Setting Boundaries

A person who feels overlooked, disrespected, used, unworthy and unimportant needs to set boundaries to protect themselves and build self-confidence.

Parents can help set boundaries by giving clear examples of proper limits and giving tips when your child feels that someone has invaded their boundaries. Let your kids understand that a boundary is not an accusation that others are hurting them. It explains how others can impact your child's life through their actions. Communicating your boundaries to others means that you are taking responsibility for your own emotions while developing a relationship built on trust and respect from the get-go.

Offensive Conduct

If you feel that someone is busy manipulating you, using you, or purposefully overstepping your boundaries, it's your job to let them know that their deeds are disrespectful and that you will not stand for it. By overlooking these negative behaviors, you are giving them permission to continue with their actions. Only you can set your boundaries, and only you can uphold them.

Parents, encourage your teenager to continue taking small steps to set emotional boundaries with their friends. It is going to need lots of practice before boundary-setting becomes easier and more natural. Remember, we all have the right to set emotional boundaries, and we don't have to explain ourselves to anybody! Healthy boundaries can mean the difference between having a healthy, positive relationship or having a hazardous, poisonous friendship. Which one would you prefer?

Embarrassment

Have you ever heard the phrase "I was so embarrassed, I nearly died!" We all have an awkward story where we said or did something so idiotic that we wished the world would open up and swallow us there and then! It doesn't matter how old you are or what you have been through. None of us are immune to embarrassment in our lives.

Even though we all have loads of stories to tell and many of us can laugh at the situation now, when it happened, we just wanted to disappear in a puff of smoke.

So how do you survive such an instance?

Don't Make it a Big Deal

Nine out of ten times, we over-exaggerate everything all the time. At that moment, you feel like the biggest fool on earth, but in hindsight, you actually realize that it wasn't so serious after all. If you have the guts to share your story with your mates, you might actually chuckle yourself! It's really okay to be embarrassed, and it's even better to share your story with your close, trusted friends. They will probably admire your honesty, applaud that you had the guts to share it with them, and trust you with one of their humiliating stories.

Sharing your story of mortification just proves to others that you are human too. Sometimes a moment of shame can be helpful because it teaches us to prepare for another similar event in the future.

Don't Apologize

Why do we continue to say sorry even if we didn't do anything intentionally? Why is shame directly linked to embarrassment? Many of us feel a deep sense of shame when we are embarrassed, which makes things so much worse. Apologizing is actually not required. Think about it. What is your reason for apologizing? Isn't it just a natural response to feelings of humiliation? If your friend walks into the bathroom while on the toilet, why do you feel the need to say sorry? After all, it was their fault, wasn't it? These things happen, and in reality, you didn't do anything wrong!

Why do we need to apologize to get back "to normal?" Will our apology take the moment away? No! In fact, you might actually feel worse because you are both paying attention to that uncomfortable event again. So, stop saying sorry already and move on already, dammit! Don't dwell on it, don't obsess over it, and just laugh it off!

Fear is Fine

Feelings of anxiety are normal after an embarrassing moment. Especially if it happens in front of someone you respect, like, or loathe, fear could keep you from moving on, though, so even if the event sticks with you for a while, you need to tell yourself that it's crucial to move on regardless of what it takes! Fear is natural, and it might come from an honest place, but that doesn't mean you can allow it to rule your life.

If you don't face your fears, you will be stuck in quicksand. We all have fears, and it doesn't make you weird because you find it difficult to deal with. It takes true strength to acknowledge your fears and to take the necessary steps to heal, but with the belief in yourself and the knowledge that we all have things that keep us up at night, you can conquer them and move on.

Perfect Imperfection

When we feel embarrassed, we sometimes believe that we did not reach the standards we set for ourselves. If you learn a valuable lesson from your failures, you actually have the potential to push yourself toward greater heights of success. Many teens stop trying to be a perfectionist because unflawed excellence is just unattainable. We have to accept that we are mere mortals that make mistakes and do awkward things every now and then. Nothing will ever be perfect, and you have to accept the fact that you are guaranteed to have uncomfortable moments in your life. You can either move past those moments or hide from your mistakes. It's your choice.

Try Again

Embarrassing moments must never hold you back in life! As long as you continue to try again, you are a champion. Only losers quit. Even if it means you have to do the same thing again, and the chances are that something might go wrong, you can keep your head held high because you know in your heart that you gave it your all.

Self-Control

Rick and Jack are best buddies at school. They met in preschool already when Jack decided to dump a bucket of sand on Rick's head. After a lot of tears and a few toddler meltdowns, the two became inseparable.

Rick is a calm, relaxed 'go with the flow' kind of guy, while Jack is high-strung and always having some type of crisis. They handle situations completely differently.

Why?

We Choose To

You would think that we can't help how we feel. If we are angry, we lash out. If we are sad, we cry, and if we feel frustrated, we yell or punch a wall. Right? No! Wrong, wrong, wrong! Yes, we are human, and unlike robots, we have feelings, but we still have a choice as to how we will react to our situation.

The limbic system is responsible for our emotions. This area of the brain is quite large, and our ancestors used it when there were still dinosaurs on earth. It's quite animalistic and can be compared to how two dogs would fight over a bone. They show their strength by barking, growling, raising their fur, and attacking one another. This is to show dominance, and the weaker party will usually run away while the victor gets the spoils. Thus, our limbic system can hijack the levels at which we respond emotionally to situations, but we can change this. "How in the hell am I going to change the way

I feel, you say?" By following these four steps, you can break the cycle of total overreaction.

Recognition

You need to become aware of your over-emotional state as it happens. Once you start to realize you are losing your cool, you can monitor yourself by identifying your feelings and labeling them.

Why

As soon as you have given your feelings a name, you can start to explore why you are reacting to them in the way you currently do. Ask yourself what happened? What triggered this feeling? Usually, it is how you rationalize the situation that is causing you to feel these emotions. Also, remember that your feelings overrun your morals and beliefs at that moment, which can make it even harder to control yourself.

Resolution

You have figured out what you are feeling and why you're feeling these things. Now you need to find out how to manage your emotions. The first step to changing your emotional habits is to rewire your thinking. Negative emotions lead to negative thought patterns. We are not saying you must lie to yourself and pretend as if life is just moonshine and roses. We suggest that you find other possible ways to look at your situation. Every so often, by merely knowing why you feel a specific way at a particular time, your emotions will start to weaken because knowledge can bring about comfort.

Response

This final step is tough and needs loads of practice. You must listen to your feelings to detect and recognize them, but now you must choose how you are going to respond to them to seal the deal and make this work. This is anything but easy, and many people don't want to try to make an effort, so they give up even before they begin. When you have mastered the art of managing your emotions, your life will change, and you will feel more empowered and in control. This means a happier you and a more relaxed atmosphere for those who had to live with your outbursts.

A Quick Exercise

Somebody just 'peed on your battery', and you are furious! You might find yourself in a public place surrounded by people, and the last thing you have time for is to follow the four steps mentioned above to calm down. Stop and breathe! Have a look at your surroundings. Categorize your emotions. Is it anger, irritation, fury? Are your emotions running wild out of the blue, or is it triggering a previous experience? Immediately try to find a tranquil, quiet spot for you to calm down and for your emotions to diminish. If you feel that the more you try to tell yourself to calm down, the more intense your feelings are, remove yourself from the public place, just until you have had the time to recenter yourself.

Self-Awareness

Self-awareness allows you to understand who you are, what you believe in, and what motivates you in life. It can help you to make better choices but be careful not to second guess yourself.

Self-awareness can be categorized into two separate components.

Internal Self-Awareness

This type of awareness is a process where we become aware of our own personal thoughts from an 'onlooker's' point of view. You notice that you are thinking a certain way when you look in the mirror, or you realize that you have butterflies in your stomach when you walk past a certain person. You become aware of your own self. So instead of automatic first-person responses, you are having a two-way conversation in your head.

External Self-Awareness

We start experiencing this type of awareness when we hit our teen years. We begin to see how the world perceives us. We start speculating what others think of us and how they judge our character. When you must recite a poem in class, for example, your ears become red, and you can feel your face getting hotter because you can feel everyone's eyes on you, and you are wondering how the rest of the class is going to respond to you. We also start to dress, talk, and behave a certain way to be more accepted by society or our peers.

We need both types of self-awareness to preserve our sense of self and to circumnavigate our way through difficult social relations. For example, in a discussion with friends, we need to be aware of which thoughts and feelings we should share and which ones we should keep to ourselves. We also need to be aware of how others might react to what we say, so we need to be empathetic towards others, so we don't hurt their feelings or harm them in other ways.

There is a third type of awareness called the self-conscious.

Self-Consciousness

Have you ever walked on the beach wishing you could take your shoes off to run and splash in the sea, but you are too worried about your ugly, crooked toes? Or you would love to dance in the rain, but you are scared people are going to think you are crazy. This is called self-consciousness. You purposefully avoid certain situations because you feel too embarrassed or scared that others around you might judge you. We all have something about ourselves that we don't like and wish we could change, which is normal. There are people who can be so self-aware that they experience anxiety attacks or severe stress because of their uncertainties.

Extreme self-consciousness can become so bad that some people don't even want to leave their house. Their concerns about what others think of them can cause so much anxiety that they become total recluses. Another major negative consequence of extreme self-consciousness is a social anxiety disorder. When someone is too self-conscious, it does not only make their fears worse. It can also cause them to think that other people are judging them when in reality, those in question aren't even paying attention to them at all.

So How Can You Become Less Self-conscious?

The number one step to overcoming this problem is to realize that the outside world is not scrutinizing your every move. It does not care what you wear or who you hang with. The rest of the globe is too concerned with their own lives than to worry about yours! Stop 'reading the situation.' It's all in your head! What proof do you have that others are saying what you think they are? You are the one overanalyzing everything, not them.

Look at the rest of the world. What are they doing? Listen to what they are saying and actually observe the situation instead of making things up in your mind. Direct your attention towards others instead of inwards towards yourself.

These are mere suggestions, but if you feel that your anxiety issues are still bothersome and inhibiting you from living life, you should ask your parents to go and see a professional.

Chapter 6

The Others

There are so many different personalities in the world, and some people are just not that nice. It's important to identify them and the negative ways they can influence situations. By recognizing these pitfalls, negative areas, or unpleasant people, we can make better decisions in social settings as well as other areas of our life in general. Don't forget that you are not alone in this cruel world. Many of us are affected by this negativity, but if you allow your little light to shine bright, you can scare away the darkness for yourself and others around you.

Victimization is not just a high school dilemma that "nerds" have to face. Many people have been victimized or persecuted by others in their adult years too. It can happen at home, at school, and work. Nobody is exempt from bullying.

There are two types of bullies. Bully 'A' enjoys hurting weaker people because it gives them a sense of power, while bully 'B' uses these tactics because they are insecure and have trouble at home. It doesn't matter why kids or adults bully others, it's not acceptable, and it should be stopped right in its tracks.

What Does Bullying Mean?

A bully uses aggression and intimidation to exert power over others. They generally target people who are smaller, weaker, and more self-conscious. Sometimes vulnerable kids tend to idolize a bully because they feel safe in their presence, or they want to possess the "strength" that the bully has over others.

Bullies harass people through:

- Coercion
- Gossip and deceit
- Intimidation
- Force
- Abuse
- Deliberate segregation

Not all bullies attack you physically. Many try to intimidate people through their size and threats of physical harm, but most use gossip, teasing and insults to hurt their targets. Adults who are seen as bullies at work will usually spread false accusations and use smear campaigns to target their co-workers.

The one thing all bullies have in common is humiliation. They want their targets to feel insecure or have a low sense of self-worth, to feel superior.

Why Do People Bully?

There's no single cause or motive for why people bully, but many of them do so because they feel unconfident, powerless, or scared in their own lives.

Some kids bully to gain popularity, while others use these tactics to win a disagreement. For many of them, violence is all they know, and that's why they physically hurt others because they get abused at home. They might not know any other way to deal with conflict or to get their needs met.

Some bullies are spoilt brats who were never told "no," and other bullies lack empathy, are jealous, or were born with egotistical traits.

Teens who are victims of bullies can:

- Become isolated
- Have suicidal thoughts
- Withdraw from the world entirely
- Develop eating disorders
- Drop out of school
- Develop mental or emotional disorders

Are You Born a Bully?

Nobody is born a bully; they also didn't just wake up one day and decide that now they're going to start harming others. It is learned behavior. Aggression and hostility might be genetic, but most of their traits are environmentally influenced. They have seen or experienced bullying in their own life and decided to mimic this behavior.

The Bully Categories

Our tormenters don't fit into one neatly labeled box. They each have their own unique reason to bully others, and their methods differ as well. Some intimidators will have traits from each category, while others won't exhibit any of these behaviors.

The Gang of Bullies

They are too scared to take people on alone, so they band together to target their victims. They generally don't have much in common and wouldn't even have been friends if it wasn't for their joint desires to hurt others. They sometimes see themselves as a gang and usually stay in a specific area that they call their turf. Their only mission in life is to show others their power, the control they have, and to dominate the weak.

The Social Bully

These guys have poor self-esteem but cover it up by portraying an exaggerated, inflated self-confidence. They are usually jealous of their victims and love to slander, taunt, or verbally abuse others. In the beginning, they pretend as if they care about you and want to help, but actually, they have their knife out, ready to stab you in the back the minute you turn away!

The Confident Bully

Nothing and no one has bigger egos than the confident bully. They think they are the bees' knees, the cat's meow, and cooler than ice. They enjoy physical harassment and show no empathy ever. They feel superior, and not even an authority figure can intimidate them.

The Armoured Bully

This class of bully is almost like a rhino. They have developed a thick skin so nothing can penetrate through it, but this is just a character they portray. The armored bully has a soft heart, but their mean exterior makes sure others avoid them in fear of being harassed.

The Relational Bully

They are the popular kids in school. They can be class captain, head of the football team, and the lead in every school play. Everybody adores them, and they have loads of friends. Their strength lies in their popularity as they can choose who runs in the 'upper-class' school circles. By excluding, isolating, and ostracizing others, they maintain their control.

They love to spread rumors and gossip to keep their popularity and will do anything to remain the head of the "in crowd."

The Serial Bully

Yes, you read right, and yes, they are exactly like serial offenders. Once they have tasted power, they will always go and look for a new victim to torture, chasing that original high they felt initially. Just like serial wrongdoers, the people around them see them as sweet, charming, and charismatic. Yet behind the mask they put on for the rest of the world lies a cold, calculated terror who loves to inflict emotional pain on their victims over long periods of time. They are super manipulators, can lie with a straight face, and will usually bully someone when they are 100% sure they won't get caught.

The Hyper Bully

Shame this type of harasser is generally on the 'lower side' of the intelligence spectrum and uses their fists to win arguments. They have no clue when it comes to socializing and will pick a fight with someone for attention.

The Bullied Bully

You should pity this bully. They are a clear-cut example of growing up in a violent environment and acting upon what they know. Their parents, siblings, or housemates use violence at home to sort things out, and because they feel completely helpless, they try to exert their power onto their victims.

Tactics Used to Bully

There are several sorts of bullying techniques and methods used to intimidate victims.

Corporal Bullying

This is the most 'old school' form of bullying. Everybody thinks of this type of intimidation when they hear the word bully. It transpires when people use their physical strength to control someone else. Bullies don't necessarily have to be bigger, stronger, or fitter than their peers to hurt them physically. Most humans hate conflict and will not fight back. Knowing this, the bully uses it to their advantage. It is the easiest to spot because of wounds or abrasions, so if you notice someone trying to cover up their injuries, ask them if they are being bullied.

Vocal Bullying

Name-calling insults and abusive statements are the tools and weapons of choice these types of bullies use to bring about shame. They target quiet kids or students with learning difficulties and special needs who find it hard to defend themselves or who can't hit back with a nasty comment. Victims of these bullies will rather die than tell a parent or an authority figure what is going on, and it is extremely difficult to spot. The problem is that verbal insults can leave permanent internal wounds that can affect victims for the rest of their lives.

Emotive Bullying

The cool crowd uses these tactics to ostracize one of their peers by lowering their social status. They will kick the victim out of the crowd and make sure that the rest of the school ignores them. This can leave them sitting alone at lunch tables, during a break, and even booted from extra-curricular activities. This kind of social manipulation is so cold and calculated that it can leave the victim feeling lonely and completely isolated. This is social suicide, and for a teen, this hurts more than any physical or emotional injury.

Bias Bullying

Anybody who makes fun of someone's race, religious beliefs, outer appearance, or sexual orientation is classified as a prejudicial bully. This type of harassment is actually very dangerous because it can escalate from simple name-calling to physical attacks and hate crimes. Some victims have been killed because of discrimination, so parents and authority figures need to keep a serious eye out for this form of exploitation among teens.

Sexual Bullying

It is not just girls who fall victim to this; many boys also suffer from being sexually harassed. Any form of physical, emotional, or mental attack in an erotic manner where the perpetrator tries to humiliate or shame their target can be classified as sexual bullying.

It also doesn't just include physical sexual exploitation either. A girl calling another female a slut or promiscuous or a boy who makes fun of a smaller teen calling him a fag is also guilty of sexual harassment.

There are many different forms that this kind of bullying can take. Physically harming someone in a sexual way, rude remarks, name-calling, obscene language or gestures, and unwanted touching all fall under this category.

Cyber Bullying

Bullying has now gone virtual, and many kids get victimized online. These days you can get bullied in your own home through social media platforms, forums, or chat rooms. Although most of these platforms forbid cyberbullying tactics, many kids just harass their targets in another way on another platform. Report bullies to the right authorities immediately so the harasser can be booted off the site. They have no right to harm others.

Onlookers and bystanders often suffer, too. Many teens who witness instances of bullying might feel remorseful or ashamed for not defending their friends. Bullying can lower morale and increase absenteeism at school. It is also not easy for victims to stand up against a bully, and it must reach a point of utterly unbearable torture before they speak up. They fear even more ridicule from their schoolmates for dragging an authority figure in to 'fight their battles for them. Many kids who have not experienced bullying don't understand how it can affect the victim and feel that the victim is just too weak to stand up for themselves.

What to Do?

Spectators can play an important role when it comes to ending bullying. Instead of looking the other way, they can take the initiative by backing up the target when they report specific accounts to the right people in power.

Bullies must suffer the consequences of their actions. If they get disciplined correctly, they might gain insight into their behavior and can start to address their own issues. For example, where they learned their behavior and what impact their conduct has on others. By protecting a bully, we do them an injustice because we stop them from getting the much needed help they require to change.

If you are the one being bullied, you can try to tell an authority figure or your parents. We know that you would rather dunk your head in a pot of hot oil than have your parents involved, but you should consider it if it's affecting your whole life.

Bullies thrive on humiliation. They love to rattle your cage, watching you sweat and tremble in fear. They don't expect you to just walk off and ignore their insults. It will make them confused and throw them off guard, which is what you want. Hold your head up high while you make your exit. It shows that you don't fear them, and they have nothing to intimidate you with without fear. Even if you have to force yourself to put one foot in front of the other, do it! They will be the one who looks like a fool.

Never try to fight back, even if you have a black belt in karate or taekwondo. Someone is going to get hurt, and even if you have fantasized over knocking their teeth out, you will get into trouble. The last thing you want is to be seen as the bully. If you do feel high levels of aggression towards the perpetrator, expend that energy somewhere else. Go for a jog or hit the punching bag at your school gym while imagining their face.

This is going to sound stupid; we know but have you tried to talk to the bully? Explain how they make you feel and point out what areas of their behavior hurt you. This is only recommended if someone is teasing you. They might find it funny and don't have a clue that their comments are harming you so badly.

If none of these tips work, you need to strategize. Steer clear from places where the bully or group of bullies can catch you alone. Only move in groups. If they can't get you alone, they can't inflict any harm. Take another route to school or home if you know that they have to use the same pathway. It might add a few extra minutes to your daily route, but it's worth it if you don't come home with a new blue shiner.

Join bullying or violence prevention programs at school or your local community center. If there isn't one in your neighborhood, do some research and start your own program.

Parents,

It's your job to protect your child, so look for these warning signs in your teen if you suspect bullying:

- Not wanting to go to school

- Faking illness to stay at home
- Isolating in their room
- Eating or sleeping disorders
- Bad grades

Trolls

Why do you want to talk about those creatures with funny multi-colored poofy haircuts who burst into song while they are strolling through the magic forest? Well, you are almost right. We do want to talk about funny creatures in magic realms, but these trolls live in cyberspace.

Cyber trolls are people who deliberately attack people online by posting hostile remarks, content, or images. Usually, victims of trolls get criticized for their principles, opinions, views, or looks.

Many teens confuse trolls with cyberbullies. They do use the same tactics, but a troll doesn't need to know you to attack you. Their main goal is to target people on social media platforms like Twitter, Facebook, YouTube to attract attention and interrupt conversations. The more people they can upset, the happier they become.

A cyberbully has a personal vendetta against their target and knows them from school, the neighborhood, or groups of friends. A troll has no idea who they are taunting. They pick a random profile. Trolls aren't out to harm you emotionally by humiliating you. They want a reaction from the community, not you. Any attention is good attention for a troll, and the more people react, the more satisfied they are and the more rubbish they will continue to post.

Identifying a Troll

Trolling can occur at any time. The one minute you are posting a picture of your birthday cake, and the next minute you are being threatened out of nowhere.

Once a troll has you in their sight, they will follow your every move. They will go through every comment or post to see what they can use as ammunition against you. They want to disrespect you and damage your reputation.

They will accuse you of terrible, atrocious behavior. They will use your own words against you and will try to break you. They warp your statements and try to make you doubt yourself. Their mission is absolute online destruction and character assassination. They will call you crazy, a kitten hater, a bunny boiler, anything they can think of to let others think you are a horrible person.

The more you or others online engage with them, the more pleased they are. They don't care about right or wrong. They care about misunderstandings and disorder.

Trolls do not adhere to online rules or social media guidelines. As soon as they get booted off a site, they will return as a new character, like choosing another avatar for their game.

Trolls make use of profanity and derogatory comments called 'flaming.' This intensifies their attack and causes the target more disgust. They know how deep words can cut, which is what they want to do.

They will post comments at an alarming rate. If you start to communicate with them, they will not leave you alone for a second.

Getting Over a Troll Attack

The first thing you need to get or understand is that you are not alone, special, or a misfit. You were not chosen out of a million people because of your looks, personality, beliefs, or views. You were the first, best profile they opened.

There is nothing wrong with you, so it's fine to feel upset and emotional, but don't beat yourself up or try to change in any way! Block the bastard and move on. If they come back as someone else, just hit the block or report button again. You will infuriate them by not responding, and eventually, they will go look for a new victim to torment. If they continue to pop up on your profile, take a break from the internet for a bit. Trolls need feedback. If you are offline, they won't hang around for too long. Trolls want to cause emotional damage, leaving you with yucky feelings. Talk to someone who can help you move on from this horrible experience. Try not to dwell on their comments, pictures, or posts. It is hurtful, but that's why they do it, to upset and offend you.

Social Media

Social media has become a huge part of humankind. Our parents were not brought up with the internet, and it can be quite intimidating for them to know that we spend so much time on our mechanical gadgets. They don't understand that we can use technology to connect to online gaming competitions, chatrooms, social media, websites to help with homework, as well as news sites that keep us up to date with happenings around the entire world.

We use it to have fun, make new friends, and maintain relationships. We can share similar interests with like-minded people, explore and develop new hobbies, etc. The internet has become an extension of our identities and our day-to-day lives. For some teens, it's a means of support, for example, those with a disability or a medical condition, LGBTQI teens, or kids who come from specific cultural backgrounds. We can link up no matter where we are and can help one another through difficulties or trying times in our lives.

Other benefits include:

- Sharing educational content and learning as a group
- Exploring our creativity through taking, editing, and posting photos and videos or even designing new websites or games
- Learning coding or expanding our career options by sourcing more information
- Gaining knowledge and skills
- We can connect with medical, emotional, and mental professionals

Risks might include:

- Exposure to inappropriate, age-restricted content like violence, sex, and child pornography
- Sharing personal information with stalkers or criminals
- Financial scams
- Cyberbullies

We know that our parents can worry about a lot, but social media safety is, unfortunately, something you guys need to discuss and reach a compromise that makes everyone happy.

There are several reasons why your parents think social media is dangerous. They have also read and heard the stories of abductions, bodies found in sewers, or teens just dropping off the face of the earth.

Before you look at the roof and ask for patience, keep in mind that a few guidelines are much better than a list of dos and don'ts.

Keep Your Privacy Private

Ask your parents to join you when you change your privacy settings on your social media platforms. You might not realize it, but the default settings still give strangers access to your posts, location, and account. Have you ever considered predators recognizing the mountain behind you in a selfie? Or a street name on a pole in your profile pic? It might sound extreme, but believe me, these things are real concerns.

Make sure that your social profile is set to only friends seeing your posts instead of the public. Even "friends of friends" can be potential stalkers because you can't be sure that your mates' privacy settings are as secure as yours.

Friend requests are super. We love it when our friend count or follower list increases, but if you don't know them, rather decline the request. Why would a complete stranger with a profile pic of a kitten choose you to be their friend? Think about it. That's definitely fishy.

Your online safety can be compromised through the personal information you allow others to see. Don't add your phone number, your house address, your school, or places you like to hang to every post the public has access to. Keep it private or change your settings, so your close friends are the only ones who have access to this information.

Admit it, we can sometimes be impulsive and reckless when it comes to posting stuff, and occasionally, we regret it afterward, but then it could be too late. Teenage girls are especially vulnerable to stalking and cyber predators.

You have to approach any online friends who you met on social media as a potential threat; even if you think you know everything about them, they could be catfishing you!

Body Image

Ask any teen about their body, and they are guaranteed to tell you one or two things they dislike about themselves. Adolescents regularly deal with substantial pressures to live up to unrealistic physical ideals. They have distorted ideas of what beauty is and how their bodies should look, their ideal weight, and what type of build they are supposed to have. Their pursuit of a "perfect" body can take a hefty toll on their confidence and self-esteem.

Reasons For a Negative Body Image

The way you feel in your own skin during your teen years can be all-consuming. If you don't like what you see in the mirror, you will permanently be worried about how your clothes sit on you, is a part of your body sticking out without you noticing, or do your friends feel ashamed to be seen with you in public?

Social media and images in glossy magazines promote the idea that we all have to be super thin or ripped. These are all such unrealistic ideals. Because we have different body shapes and our genes have a lot to do with this, we just can't help it. We were born that way.

Our peers can force us to dress a certain way, wear specific makeup, or have our hair cut in a specific style before they accept us into their group. Even our parents might be striving towards an unattainable body shape ideal, and their judgments can also harm your already shaky self-esteem.

If we have a negative body image, we are susceptible to low self-esteem, depression, eating disorders, and risks of illness linked to taking medications to suppress our appetites or steroids so we can bulk up in the gym. Some of us are already saving our pocket money for plastic surgery so our friends can admire us. It doesn't matter how much surgery we have to change ourselves; the reality is that we will never be satisfied, and we will always chase that dream of perfectionism.

How Can Parents Help?

Parents who are worried about their teen's negative self-image should talk to them and try to encourage self-acceptance by using positive praise. For example, tell them how beautiful their hair is and talk about their other strengths, soothing voice, gorgeous eyes, tenacity, and fighting spirit. Anything goes, as long as they realize that they have other talents and positive attributes that they can be proud of.

Set a good example. The way you look at your body or talk about yourself can influence your child. Remind them that exercise and a balanced diet are great for their health and will also add years to their lives.

Remind your adolescent that their body is busy going through major changes during puberty and that starving themselves could cause permanent neurological damage, which could be irreversible.

Finally, show them unconditional love. Maybe all they need is a big hug and some positive affirmations to lift their spirits.

When to Consult a Doctor

If your kid is obsessed with their body, regardless of what you say, it might be time to go to a professional. They will be able to give your teen the necessary tools to counteract all that social pressure and to feel good about their body.

Chapter 7

Recognition

I was caught off guard when one of the 'mean girls' approached me and told me that they loved my scarf. "Why, thank you," I replied, but just before I wanted to compliment her, she added: "It's just a pity that it doesn't hide your thick neck. "I felt my tummy tie into a knot and ran to the bathroom, fearing that I might vomit in front of the entire school.

Emotional Triggers

Why did that comment upset me so much? Usually, I don't give a damn what the 'meddlers' say, but today that girl managed to ruin me emotionally. This is called an emotional trigger. Sometimes memories of past events, experiences, or fears can cause a reaction that we did not expect.

I was teased as a young kid because of my baby fat, so immediately when she mentioned my thick neck, all those memories came flooding back, and I was that shy six-year-old again.

We go through a range of emotions every day. We can go from waking up all excited to total anxiety just before a test to floating on clouds when we know we are going to see the love of our life. How we respond to different events has to do with our current state of mind and circumstances.

Understanding your emotional triggers and knowing how to deal with them is crucial for your emotional well-being.

Why do we all have emotional triggers? When we were kids, we might have been ridiculed, rejected, treated unfairly, excluded from the elite, ignored, lied to, or challenged. This made us feel insecure and unwanted. These feelings never go away, and we push them into our subconscious. As soon as something similar occurs, these emotions get triggered, and all those negative feelings come gushing back.

The best way to identify your triggers is to become aware of when a situation produces a strong emotional response in you.

Some situations can also cause physical symptoms like:

A racing heart, sweaty palms or forehead, an upset stomach, nausea, and trembling.

As soon as you notice these physical indicators, stop whatever you are doing and reflect on what just happened and how you responded to it.

Try to trace the origin of your feelings. What happened in your past that made you feel exactly the same way then? What age are you at that moment? What exactly triggered your emotional and physical symptoms?

When we start with our assessments, we might struggle to find the link, the connection, or the reason for our trigger, but this means we have to dig a little bit deeper to find our answer. We cannot avoid or ignore these emotions; we must fight back! Try to look for patterns so that you can identify your triggers.

After you identify and acknowledge your emotional triggers, you will think all your problems are solved, but alas, you will have to do a bit more than that. Even if you can label your emotional state, it won't stop you from feeling. There is no escape or shortcut. You will have to deal with your triggers every time they arise.

So how do you respond to your triggers?

Own It

You felt, identified, labeled, and now you have to own them! Remember you are allowed to feel this way, agro, sad, scared. You might feel any or all of them, and that's just dandy.

Remind yourself that your emotions might be the same, but your circumstances aren't. If your lover comes back from work and just falls on the couch not listening to your questions about their day, you might be taken back to your childhood when you felt your parents never listened to you.

Great! You felt ignored. You realized that you were feeling unheard, and you could trace it back to why. So well done, you just passed your first trigger exam!

Look at the Differences

Now you need to remind yourself that there are differences between the past and your present situation, but do it with love and compassion, no judgment.

This cue can help you regain control and realize that you have the choice to respond differently.

Take a Breather

Give yourself some space. Put some distance between the two of you so you can cool down and get your bearings.

Your main aim is not to sidestep the situation that triggered you. It's so you can regain control over your emotions and think rationally.

After you calm down, you can return to the situation that triggered you with a better mindset.

See Both Sides of the Coin

We don't want to hurt our friends or our loved ones. Maybe your partner ignored you because they were wrapped up in their own head. There might have been issues at work or in their family life. Perhaps they just had a horrible day and also need to process their emotions. We all deal with our feelings in our own habitual ways, so try to understand their point of view.

Communicate

We know when we get upset or angry, some of us clam up and expect the guilty party who angered us to read our minds. Guess what? They can't! Start your conversation with "I feel" statements. This shows that you are taking responsibility for your feelings and explaining the reason for your behavior. Now ask them why they behaved the way they did and see if you guys can come to a conclusion.

The Cure

Finding the root or reason for your triggers is one thing, but becoming mindful of your behaviors is something completely different. You need to become aware of your emotions and then change your reaction as soon as you have identified your feelings. This will be a long and tedious process, but in the end, it will all be worth it. Why not make it your mission to spoil yourself when you managed to pull it off. We all work harder when we have a goal to reach.

Leave those toxic relationships behind and move on. Those around you can't be held responsible for your actions, but they need to be held accountable for theirs; if they influence you negatively and only bring out the worst in you, put on some serious-looking boots and kick them to the curb!

Writing your emotional triggers down on a daily basis is a useful tool to reveal patterns and track your success. You can also figure out what works and what doesn't. A feelings journal isn't as "cliché" as you think. It can be a great healing instrument.

If you feel that your triggers are becoming too much to bear, seek professional help. A therapist has the means and the know-how to deal with your troubles. This is what they were trained for and why

Awful memories and dreadful events can cause damage in anyone's life, but if you can manage triggers efficiently, you can reduce your anguish and increase your self-respect.

Anxiety

Grace is a typical teen. She loves to play hockey, enjoys playing her guitar, and likes to go out with her friends on the weekends. Her mom Samantha is a typical parent with a twist. She worries like most moms, but she starts to panic as soon as Grace leaves the house. She wonders if Grace will make it to the movies alive. Will she be robbed, attacked, held hostage, or worse be killed? It is normal to be concerned about your kids, but in Samantha's case, these uncertainties are causing anxiety, and it is ruling her whole life!

Anxiety is a normal emotional response that is linked to human survival. It is the body's alarm that goes off when our mind perceives something as dangerous or threatening. When this warning system kicks in, we start to have a heightened physical awareness. Our hearts beat faster, we tense up, we breathe heavier, our hands start to shake, and we begin sweating. This is the body's way to get ready to run or fight for its life. It is caused by an adrenaline injection as well as a release of other chemicals to ensure a swift getaway. Our bodies respond first to fear, with the mind that follows a few seconds after. It's automatic, and when our natural warning system kicks in, it can help us to dodge dangerous situations.

Typical Anxiety

Every human being on earth gets anxious every now and again. We can feel restless, edgy, fearful, and terrified when we realize we are stuck in a hazardous situation or dangerous circumstances. While fear is an emotion linked to danger, feelings of anxiety are connected to anticipated threats.

Typical anxiousness can include mild feelings of unease or nervousness. Still, intense anxiety leads to sure panic, dread, and such an overwhelming feeling of fear that it can intimidate the person who suffers from it so badly that it affects their lives negatively.

When we are faced with any new or unfamiliar situations, our natural instincts kick in, and we become nervous. People who suffer from extreme anxiety can become so distressed that they avoid anything they perceive as a "potential" threat. They will stop going to social gatherings in fear of being embarrassed in public. They won't try to make any friends because of their rejection issues, and they might stop living life because they are terrified of making a mistake or not fitting in.

A dose of normal anxiety keeps us alert, focused, and ready to take on any potential threats. It can even increase our performance, but extreme anxiety levels can interfere with our lives to such a degree that we become scared of everything.

Conditions and Disorders

An anxiety disorder can be described as a mental condition that turns your irrational fears into an intense, endless cycle that preoccupies and overpowers your judgment. These types of disorders can affect people of all ages from all walks of life.

If these feelings of dread and terror occur too often, are too intense, are blown out of proportion, and affect a person's daily life and happiness, it's time to seek professional help. There are various disorders, and each one has its own set of symptoms.

Generalized anxiety is an unreasonable number of fears about numerous things like school, health, general safety, or even the future. People suffering from this always think that the worst is about to happen to them.

Phobias are such powerful fears of harmless situations that can cause people to avoid the things they are so scared of.

Social phobia includes strong anxiety triggered by any kind of social situation where they need to talk to a group of people or even just have a conversation with someone they find intimidating.

Obsessive-compulsive disorder or OCD is a form of anxiety where the person suffers from obsessive thoughts and compulsions. They will have strange habits like knocking on the door three times, and if they add or miss a knock, they will obsess and fear unnatural consequences to arise.

Panic attacks are abrupt, intense physical symptoms that can cause the body to overreact, for example, not being able to breathe when they feel overwhelmed.

Anxiety disorders or any of the other conditions mentioned can affect a sufferer so badly that it steals their joy in life. People who have high levels of anxiety are permanently on guard feel completely misunderstood, and their irrational fears can cause them to live a life of isolation and loneliness.

Some blame themselves and feel too embarrassed or ashamed to ask for help. The good news is that treatment can help them feel better and live a normal, happy life.

Stress Management

We throw the word 'stress' around so easily. When our toenails are painted the wrong color, we are so stressed. When we can't find the right shoes to go with our outfit, we stress, and when we think the guy or girl we have a crush on noticed our new pimple, we stress. It's fine when you feel a bit anxious over a major test you need to write or if you are rehearsing for your ballet recital, but chronic or long-term stress is a whole different ballgame.

If left untreated, chronic or long-term stress can cause various mental and physical health problems. Our immune systems can take a huge knock, and we become more susceptible to illnesses, heart disease, blood pressure problems, heart attacks, and even obesity.

For many teens, their main cause of chronic stress is their tense home life, for example, their parents' divorce or major life changes like a new mom or dad, a stepsibling, or things like physical, drug, or alcohol abuse. School life can also cause high levels of stress. Peer pressure, social anxieties, bullies, and harsh teachers can all play a part in a teens' major strains.

As an adolescent gets older, their causes of stress can increase. Many young adults worry about fitting in at a new school. They have to deal with love loss in romantic relationships, and issues like pressure to have sex can make their anxiety levels go through the roof!

Identifying the Signs of Stress

Someone who is suffering from intense stress can present these symptoms:

Stressed-out teens can be very short-tempered and highly irritable. They can have hectic mood swings and might start arguments or physical fights for no reason. They could also act out in various ways by locking themselves in their rooms, yelling or screaming at the top of their lungs, or staying out way past their curfew.

Many youths will have sleeping disorders, sleeping too much or not at all. They can overheat or stop eating altogether, and their immune systems can be so shot that they become ill more often than usual.

Managing Stress

Physical exercise, eating healthy and adequate sleep are all brilliant stress busters. Spending some time outdoors and with loved ones are wonderful ways to get rid of unnecessary stress goblins. Talking to an adult who you trust is a great way to help reduce stress. They don't just offer an ear to listen to. Many grownups will identify with your feelings and can offer guidance. If none of these suggestions are easing your worries, it's best to go and speak to a therapist who can give you solid, guaranteed advice.

What Parents Can Do

We have to become living role models for teaching our kids how to deal with stress productively by adopting healthy habits and providing stress-management strategies. Help to become problem solvers by playing detective and asking your teen to find the root cause of their problems. Read books and other informative articles that can help your child discover their triggers and find ways how to deal with them appropriately. Get them out of that deep, dark hole of negative thinking by boosting their confidence and focusing on their positive traits. Let them dig deep to develop their own resilience to stressful situations in their lives.

Controlling Our Emotions

You must have heard the phrases "self-regulation" and "self-control," right? Surely your parents or teachers have reprimanded you by saying you need to control yourself. What do these words mean, and how do they differ?

It's easier to explain by using an example, so let's say Pete is a chocoholic, but he wants to join the track team and decided to cut down on his daily sugar fix. His friend Tony wants to buy his new girlfriend a valentine's gift, and the local sweet shop has loads of tasters to test before you choose which sweets to buy for your sweet. Pete tags along, and even though there are hundreds of chocolate tester pieces to taste, he holds himself in and manages to leave the store with his goals intact. This is called self-control, and Pete passed with flying colors!

If we take the same scenario, but instead of Pete walking past all the goodies on offer, he jumps in the tasters and gobbles up as much as he can fit into his mouth, swallowing without chewing, then turns around and accuses Tony of being a crappy friend for forcing him to walk into a temptation hut from hell, he is definitely struggling with self-regulation.

It is important to regulate and control our emotions because how we deal with them is directly linked to managing stress. If we can successfully deal with stress, we will be able to handle any typical life challenges we may face in the future. When we are unable to manage our stress levels, we have much greater difficulty trying to solve our problems and living life on life's terms.

Dr. Shanker developed a set of strategies to help people with self-regulation. His method is referred to as the "5 R's." (self-reg.ca/self-reg-101)

Reframe: Before you think that your point of view is the only correct one, it is vital to look at it from every possible angle.

Recognize: Identify if your stress is physical, emotional, cognitive, social (what you see online), or pro-social (if you stress about other people's situations). If you can recognize what you are feeling, you can deal with it in a better, healthier way.

Reduce: Find suitable strategies to decrease and minimize your stress.

Reflect: Recognize and acknowledge your feelings.

Respond: Find positive ways to increase your capacity to manage the stressful situation you are in at that moment.

Just Chill

Life is stressful enough, but during adolescence, it can be so overbearing that you feel your head is going to explode! Our days can be filled with frustration, annoying people, as well as unpleasant situations, and we are just talking about your family life! Some days are worse than others, and if you are dealing with elevated stress, you need to relax to make life more pleasant for both you and your loved ones. There are numerous relaxation tips, techniques, and suggestions out there to relieve your stress when things get so bad that all you want to do is punch everyone you come across in the face just because you can!

Deep Breathing

You must have seen someone breathing into a small brown paper bag in a movie when they are having a panic attack because aliens are taking over the world? This isn't just a humorous setup before a funny punchline. Breathing exercises are actually a form of meditation and can be very beneficial as a relaxation technique to help decrease your stress levels. People who suffer from panic attacks take rapid, shallow breaths, which tenses the body up even more. When we hyperventilate, we struggle with getting enough air, making us very edgy.

Slow, deep breaths through the diaphragm, where your focus is on breathing air into your tummy instead of your chest, is a brilliant relaxation technique that can be practiced anywhere without any help or equipment. Another method called square breathing is also good for relaxation. It entails inhaling for five seconds, holding your breath for five seconds, exhaling for five seconds, holding for another five seconds, and then repeating the exercise again from the start.

Meditation

Many of us think of bald-headed monks on icy mountain tops becoming one with the cosmos when we hear the word meditation, but it is actually just about clearing your mind of those niggling, undesirable feelings and thoughts.

There are too many ways to mention. Some mediation techniques focus on words or sounds, while others focus more on visuals like flames or a person talking you through the process. You will have to do some research to find the method that suits your personality best.

Progressive Muscle Relaxation

When we become frustrated, tense, or stressed out, we tend to clench our jaws and tighten our muscles. Our necks become stiff, and our backs might feel as if we've been hit by a truck and, sometimes, even our fingers can be tender if we stay strung out and tense. Progressive muscle relaxation is a technique where you focus on each body part, starting at your neck and working your way down to your toes. Tense up your muscles in your neck as tightly as you can, and then relax completely. Move on to your shoulders and do the same with them. Continue these exercises with each body part until you get to your toes. You will feel how those muscles relax after you complete this process.

Imagery

It sounds tricky, but it is possible to imagine yourself in a calm, tranquil place, regardless of the noise or any other distractions around you. Think of that one specific place in the world you would rather be right now. Some people call it their safe place, while others just imagine a place where they had happy memories like a forest, a beach, a waterfall, in the bush, on your bed at home, it doesn't really matter where, as long as it calms you down and relaxes you.

If you find it too difficult to focus on your own, go for guided imagery therapy sessions or download a session online. Here, a person will guide you, keep you on track and help you to stop your mind from wandering. Remember, you need to be totally immersed in your fantasy, so you must try your best to see, hear, feel, smell, and even taste whatever you're visualizing. It's going to take practice, but the more you do it, the easier it will become.

Keep on Spinning

Your little brother just got a fidget spinner, and even though you pretended that it's just a stupid kid's toy when he goes to sleep, you are secretly playing with it yourself! You love watching it spin, doing some cool tricks with it, and in a sense, this little new age spinning top is soothing the savage beast inside you, but why? The truth is we all fiddle permanently without even noticing. Some of us twiddle our thumbs, play with an elastic band or tinker with something. Fidget toys are actually very popular and in demand as a way for anxious people to relieve their edginess.

We are still not sure why and there is no concrete evidence to prove that fidget spinners calm the nerves, but many kids, teens, and adults have found this little kids' toy a magical remedy against extreme anxiety and tension.

Fiddling and fidgeting is the body's way of discharging cropped-up energy. Some of us tap our feet; some might bite their nails, while others twirl their hair. It's an automatic process, and most of us don't even register that we are doing it.

Fidget toys can help a person focus, pay more attention, calm down, and even increase their active listening skills. There are so many different kinds to choose from. Stress balls, Silly Putty, Flexi Sticks, fidget spinners, fiddle cubes, and much more! They might be different, but their end goal is the same, enhancing your listening skills and improving your learning capabilities. People who struggle with concentration actually focus better when their hands are kept busy, and these toys can soothe those who have extreme levels of anxiety and prolonged stress.

You might think of them as juvenile playthings, but fidget toys are appropriate for all ages, so go grab one for yourself and get one for mom and dad while you are at it! It will make everyone calmer, less stressed, and more relaxed.

Positive Thinking

You must have heard people talking about your inner voice? That little voice in your head that you have discussions with constantly. We talk to ourselves all the time, sometimes consciously and other times subconsciously. But we are always in conversation.

It's tough to stay positive if we continuously talk down to ourselves. Sometimes no one can hurt us as much as we can. We can wind ourselves up so badly that we become angry, irritable, frustrated, and self-defeating.

Trying to talk to ourselves in a constructive, optimistic manner is hard but definitely doable. When we begin to challenge our negative self-talk, we regain the lost power that we give away.

A good way to test the accuracy of your inner voice is to ask yourself some thought-provoking questions. They can help you gauge if your current interpretations are true or not.

Examples include:

- Are my thoughts correct?
- What evidence do I have to support my assumptions?
- Are my judgments factual, or am I jumping to conclusions?

- If I turn the situation around, can I see it in a more positive light?

Developing an optimistic outlook on life is not easy, but through positive thinking, it is possible, and with the right skills, you can become a confident, productive, happy soul. The first thing you have to do is to recognize when that inner voice of yours is spewing negative garbage about yourself and the rest of the world. Negative thoughts and words have a massive impact, so change those nasty judgments into hopeful, prolific verdicts.

It's much simpler to stay positive and motivate yourself when you have set goals for yourself. They help you to overcome difficulties and hindrances in your life. When you cruise from day to day without a future life plan, you lose focus, go backward instead of progressing and make dumb decisions. Keep in mind that you will stumble from time to time, but as long as you take responsibility for your actions, you can get back on track and move forward.

If you surround yourself with positive people, read books on becoming successful and practice positive thinking, these things are bound to rub off on you, and eventually, you will gain all the rewards of a happy life and a real bright future!

Conclusion

There are no other stages in a human's life than infancy and adolescence, whereas many physical, emotional, and mental changes occur so quickly and continually. We go through dramatic fluctuations, our hormones go haywire, and we feel uncomfortable in our own skin. We go from inexperienced babies to complete mature adults in a few years. It's not surprising at all that these massive changes make us scared, emotional, and stressed out!

As if that's not enough, we begin noticing hair in funny places, we start having feelings for others, and we get introduced to sex, social anxiety, and independence. Our brains are growing, our feet are growing, and everything in between is growing too. It is also very important for parents to notice and assess any difficulties you pick up in your teen's life that they might be facing. Peer pressure, rejection, bullies, fights, social isolation, sadness, rage, anxiety, and poor academic performance can all be reasons for your adolescent's poor social skills. Identifying and addressing these issues will help both parents and their kids develop a plan to improve behaviors and address any other challenges together.

When they are not addressed, these issues could persist and might become so severe that it has a significant impact on any social interactions, future performance, and even the ability to thrive as a grown-up.

Puberty can be a struggle, a challenge, and some of the best years of your life! You don't have to be a social butterfly or the highlight of every party to be liked by your peers. Of course, you have your own personality traits, and we don't want you to change who you are in any way, but we hope that these suggestions in this book will help you to make it just that little bit easier to interact with others. Positive relationships will help you as an individual to thrive. Well-developed social skills will also give you that much-needed confidence in your ability to approach every situation and complete any tasks more successfully. Go on, use these tips and tricks, suggestions, and recommendations to get out there and show the world a star has been born, and they are going to change this world in more ways than one!

TELL US WHAT YOU THINK!

WE REALLY HOPED YOU ENJOYED READING
INSPIRING TEENS THROUGH SOCIAL SKILLS
TO SHOW YOUR SUPPORT FOR US IN OUR QUEST HELP TEENS AND THEIR FAMILIES PLEASE GO TO
AMAZON AND LEAVE A REVIEW

To hear about any of our new books coming out visit us at
www.roundhillpress.com

References

5 tips for dealing with trolls. (n.d.). Au.reachout.com. Retrieved February 26, 2022, from https://au.reachout.com/articles/5-tips-for-dealing-with-trolls

Anxiety disorders in teenagers. (2019, February 5). Raising Children Network. https://raisingchildren.net.au/pre-teens/mental-health-physical-health/stress-anxiety-depression/anxiety-disorders

Cassada, R. (2013, December 23). Top 20 Social Networking Etiquette Tips for Teens | Psychology Today United Kingdom. Www.psychologytoday.com. https://www.psychologytoday.com/gb/blog/teen-angst/201512/top-20-social-networking-etiquette-tips-teens

Center for Parent and Teen Communication. (2020, July 16). Teens, Build a Stress Management Plan. Center for Parent and Teen Communication. https://parentandteen.com/teen-stress-management-plan/

Cherry, K. (2020a, July 14). What Is Self-Awareness? Verywell Mind; Verywellmind. https://www.verywellmind.com/what-is-self-awareness-2795023

Cherry, K. (2020b, July 27). Types of Nonverbal Communication. Verywell Mind. https://www.verywellmind.com/types-of-nonverbal-communication-2795397

Cirino, E. (2017, October 12). How to Stop Blushing for No Reason and So Much. Healthline.

https://www.healthline.com/health/how-to-stop-blushing#TOC_TITLE_HDR_1

Ford-Lanza, A. (2017, June 6). Everything You Need to Know About Fidget Toys for ADHD & Anxiety. Adapt-And-Learn. https://www.adaptandlearn.com/post/everything-you-need-to-know-about-fidget-toys-for-adhd-anxiety

Forde, J. (2017, November 22). 7 Essential Lessons on Social Media Awareness for Young Teens, Parents & Teachers. Colour My Learning. https://www.colourmylearning.com/2017/11/7-essential-lessons-on-social-media-awareness-for-young-teens-parents-teachers/

Friedman, M. (2014, May 20). Knowing Why Bullies Bully Is Key to Stopping the Trend. Psychology Today. https://www.psychologytoday.com/gb/blog/brick-brick/201405/knowing-why-bullies-bully-is-key-stopping-the-trend

Frisén, A., Jonsson, A.-K., & Persson, C. (2007). Adolescents' perception of bullying: who is the victim? Who is the bully? What can be done to stop bullying? Adolescence, 42(168), 749–761. https://pubmed.ncbi.nlm.nih.gov/18229509/

Gibson, C. (2021, May 20). How to Deal With Bullies as a Teenager. WikiHow. https://www.wikihow.com/Deal-With-Bullies-as-a-Teenager

Gordon, S. (2017, October 27). 6 Types of Bullying Every Parent Should Know About. Verywell Family; Verywellfamily. https://www.verywellfamily.com/types-of-bullying-parents-should-know-about-4153882

Grossman, D. (2019). The 5 Ws and H Guide to Communicating Virtually Anything. Yourthoughtpartner.com. https://www.yourthoughtpartner.com/blog/bid/53902/the-5-ws-and-an-h-to-communicate-virtually-anything

Hinck, M. (2017, April 13). Can Fidget Toys Help Your Child's Ability To Focus? - Health Beat. Health Beat. https://www.flushinghospital.org/newsletter/can-fidget-toys-help-your-childs-ability-to-focus/

How to Have and Hold Dazzling Conversation With Anyone: We Review 11 Science Backed Steps. (2016, January 12). Science of People. https://www.scienceofpeople.com/have-hold-conversation/

Jensen, F. E. (2021). The Teenage Brain: A Neuroscientist's Survival Guide to Raising Adolescents and Young Adults: Jensen, Frances E, Nutt, Amy Ellis: 9780062067852: Amazon.com: Books. Amazon.com. https://www.amazon.com/Teenage-Brain-Neuroscientists-Survival-Adolescents/dp/0062067850/ref=sr_1_1?keywords=the+teenage+brain&qid=1637401810&sr=8-1

Kidscape. (n.d.). Dealing with bullying. Www.kidscape.org.uk. Retrieved February 25, 2022, from https://www.kidscape.org.uk/advice/advice-for-young-people/dealing-with-bullying/

Landrón Arroyo, E. (2020, September 5). The 6 P's of Project Management. Smart Precise Solutions. https://www.smartprecisesolutions.com/2020/09/6-ps-of-project-management/

Lazzeri, G., Azzolini, E., Pammolli, A., Simi, R., Meoni, V., & Giacchi, M. V. (2014). Factors associated with unhealthy behaviours and health outcomes: a cross-sectional study among tuscan adolescents (Italy). International Journal for Equity in Health, 13(1). https://doi.org/10.1186/s12939-014-0083-5

Lyness, D. (2017). Organizing Schoolwork & Assignments (for Teens) - KidsHealth. Kidshealth.org. https://kidshealth.org/en/teens/focused.html

Lyness, D. (2018, August). Body Image and Self-Esteem. Kidshealth.org. https://kidshealth.org/en/teens/body-image.html

Makwana, B., Lee, Y., Parken, S., & Farmer, L. (2018). Selfie-Esteem: The Relationship Between Body Dissatisfaction and Social Media in Adolescent and Young Women | In-Mind. Www.in-Mind.org. https://www.in-mind.org/article/selfie-esteem-the-relationship-between-body-dissatisfaction-and-social-media-in-adolescent?gclid=Cj0KCQiAtJeNBhCVARIsANJUJ2H NirksnXUTHc5A7MthD3u9ITX0G8R7QsvFigYbiSfuen ot1mbN9AwaAtvJEALw_wcB

McMillan, L. (2021, June 9). How to Spot and Cope with Emotional Triggers. Greatist. https://greatist.com/happiness/emotional-triggers#what-are-they

Melbourne Child Psychology & School Psychology Services. (n.d.). How to Help Teenagers Develop Empathy. Www.melbournechildpsychology.com.au. Retrieved February 14, 2022, from https://www.melbournechildpsychology.com.au/blog/help-teenagers-develop-empathy/

Monke, A. (2020, September 2). 7 Simple Steps to Teach Kids to Introduce Themselves. Sunshine Parenting. https://sunshine-parenting.com/7-simple-steps-teach-kids-introduce/

Monroe, J. (2017, April 5). Positive Thinking for Teens. Newport Academy. https://www.newportacademy.com/resources/mental-health/positivity-teen-mental-health/

Morin, D. A. (2020, December 18). How To Keep A Conversation Going (With Examples). SocialPro. https://socialpronow.com/blog/the-5-best-ways-to-keep-a-conversation-going/

National Centre Against Bullying. (2021). Types of Bullying | National Centre against Bullying. Ncab.org.au. https://www.ncab.org.au/bullying-advice/bullying-for-parents/types-of-bullying/

NHS Choices. (2019). Healthy eating for teens. NHS. https://www.nhs.uk/live-well/eat-well/healthy-eating-for-teens/

Nichols, R. G., & Stevens, L. A. (2014, August). Listening to People. Harvard Business Review. https://hbr.org/1957/09/listening-to-people

Nicole. (2019, August 12). 10 Benefits Of Being Organized That Will Motivate You To Start Today. Lillies and Lashes. https://www.lilliesandlashes.com/benefits-of-being-organized/

Novak, D. (2021, September 9). How to Deal With Embarrassment. WikiHow. https://www.wikihow.com/Deal-With-Embarrassment

Nutrition and healthy food for teenagers. (2018, December 13). Raising Children Network. https://raisingchildren.net.au/teens/healthy-lifestyle/daily-food-guides/nutrition-healthy-food-teens

O' Brien, S. (2021, October 21). How to Introduce Yourself. WikiHow. https://www.wikihow.com/Introduce-Yourself

O'Rourke, L. (2019, March 7). Does Your Teen Drink Enough Water? Find out Now. Pardon Me My Crown Slipped. https://www.pardonmemycrownslipped.com/hydration-why-its-so-important-for-teens/

Peper, J. S., & Dahl, R. E. (2013). The Teenage Brain. Current Directions in Psychological Science, 22(2), 134–139. https://doi.org/10.1177/0963721412473755

Pietro, S. (2016, January 29). Teens and Sleep: The Cost of Sleep Deprivation. Child Mind Institute; Child Mind Institute. https://childmind.org/article/happens-teenagers-dont-get-enough-sleep/

Price, C. (2018, January 8). Strengthening Your Teen's Social and Conversation Abilities. Hey Sigmund. https://www.heysigmund.com/strengthening-teens-social-conversation-abilities/

Raising Children Network. (2017, December 11). Brain development: teenagers. Raising Children Network. https://raisingchildren.net.au/pre-teens/development/understanding-your-pre-teen/brain-development-teens

Regan, S. (2021, June 28). Are You Good At Reading Social Cues? See If You Recognize These 17 Common Ones.

Mindbodygreen. https://www.mindbodygreen.com/articles/social-cues-types-and-how-to-read-them

Relaxation Skills for Teens. (2019, January 21). Newport Academy. https://www.newportacademy.com/resources/well-being/relaxation-skills-for-teens/

Roche, S. (2019). Why is listening important? Alchemyformanagers.co.uk. https://www.alchemyformanagers.co.uk/topics/tv8zhuMZpZEzsgNc.html

S, V., B.Sc, B.A., & Morin, D. A. (2019, December 18). 14 Tips to Be Less Self-Conscious (If Your Mind Goes Blank). SocialPro. https://socialpronow.com/blog/less-self-conscious/

Self-Reg 101. (n.d.). Self-Reg. Retrieved March 2, 2022, from https://self-reg.ca/self-reg-101/

Selva, J. (2018, January 5). How to Set Healthy Boundaries: 10 Examples + PDF Worksheets. PositivePsychology.com. https://positivepsychology.com/great-self-care-setting-healthy-boundaries/

Sloat, S. (n.d.). How to end a conversation: 2 science-backed methods. Inverse. Retrieved February 24, 2022, from https://www.inverse.com/mind-body/ending-conversations-is-so-hard-study

Soghomonian, I. (2019, September 23). Boundaries - Why are they important? The Resilience Centre. https://www.theresiliencecentre.com.au/boundaries-why-are-they-important/

Somerville, L. H. (2013). The Teenage Brain. Current Directions in Psychological Science, 22(2), 121–127. https://doi.org/10.1177/0963721413476512

Stanford Children's Health. (2019). The Growing Child: Teenager (13 to 18 Years). Stanfordchildrens.org. https://www.stanfordchildrens.org/en/topic/default?id=the-growing-child-adolescent-13-to-18-years-90-P02175

Storm, S. (2017, September 23). The Teen Struggles of Each Personality Type. Psychology Junkie. https://www.psychologyjunkie.com/2017/09/23/teenage-struggles-every-myers-briggs-personality-type/MBTI, Myers-Briggs Type Indicator, and Myers-Briggs are trademarks or registered trademarks of the Myers and Briggs Foundation, Inc., in the United States and other countries.

The Importance of Physical Activity in Youth | Little Tikes Commercial. (2019, October 9). LTC. https://littletikescommercial.com/blog/physical-fitness-teens/?lang=can

What's Going On in the Teenage Brain? (2019). HealthyChildren.org. https://www.healthychildren.org/English/ages-stages/teen/Pages/Whats-Going-On-in-the-Teenage-Brain.aspx

wikiHow. (2007, February 26). End a Conversation Without Being Rude. WikiHow; wikiHow. https://www.wikihow.com/End-a-Conversation-Without-Being-Rude

Printed in Great Britain
by Amazon

eea57bc9-d348-4b43-a53f-1cf277059665R01